The Cultural World of the Apostles

Edward A. Scully

Nov/2001

The Cultural World of the Apostles

The Second Reading, Sunday by Sunday
Year A

John J. Pilch

THE LITURGICAL PRESS
Collegeville, Minnesota

www.litpress.org

1   2   3   4   5   6   7   8   9

Library of Congress Cataloging-in-Publication Data

Pilch, John J.
   The cultural world of the apostles: the second reading, Sunday by Sunday, year A / John J. Pilch.
      p. cm.
   Includes bibliographical references.
   ISBN 0-8146-2726-9 (alk. paper)
   1. Bible. N.T. Epistles–Liturgical use. 2. Bible. N.T. Revelation–Liturgical use. 3. Bible. N.T. Epistles–History of contemporary events. 4. Bible. N.T. Revelation–History of contemporary events. 5. Middle East–Civilization–To 622. I. Title.

BS2635.55 .P55 2001
227'.067–dc21

00-052042

Dedicated with esteem and affection to

Dr. Jadwiga Małgorzata Rakowska

Friend and Cultural Informant

Contents

Introduction

During a recent extended visit—my third—to Poland, I realized that I was suffering culture shock. The discovery surprised me. I was born in America of first-generation American parents, but my first language was Polish. I am fluent in that language. My formal education included fourteen years of the study of the Polish language, history, culture, and literature. In Poland, people often ask, "When did you return to Poland?" or "How long have you lived in America." They are surprised to learn that I was born in America.

As I reflected upon and analyzed my shocking experiences, it became clear to me that the pain was caused because I was misunderstanding and misinterpreting my experiences. I was insufficiently aware of the melody of the spoken language that gives nuance to spoken words. I also failed to notice nonverbal cues. Gradually I realized that this is a high-context culture; that is, people assume and take many things for granted because every one is socialized to know what is expected in each interpersonal interaction. In contrast, my own low-context American culture has socialized me to expect everything to be spelled out in great detail. In brief, I realized that I do not know the Polish social system very well, for it is the social system that gives meaning to language and human experience. The Polish-American social system in which I was socialized is somewhat helpful but mostly inadequate for Poland.

This visit differed from the others in that I was the guest of a native Pole. She served as a guide and informant. She explained and interpreted my puzzling experiences even though she didn't witness many of them. She recommended a newly published dictionary written for foreigners. I consulted it often during our postdinner discussions to clarify for myself nuances in this highly inflected language. Moreover, the dictionary pointed out that much of my vocabulary is "literary." In modern Poland, a new and different vocabulary has developed. I came to appreciate the value of a native cultural informant or guide.

People whose cultural background is not Mediterranean or Middle- Eastern should expect the same kind of shocking experiences when they read the Bible. If reading the Bible is not a jarring experience, that could be a clue that the reader is imposing her or his culture upon the people on the pages of their English translations. Such a reading tends to make those people "just like us." Any contemporary experience with people from others cultures should make one quite aware of the fact that "they" are not "just like us."

In my three-volume series *The Cultural World of Jesus: Sunday by Sunday* (Collegeville: The Liturgical Press, 1995–97), I tried to serve my readers as a cultural informant or guide. No, I am not a native of the Mediterranean world, but my colleagues in The Context Group and I have spent a good portion of our careers studying the writings of "ancient informants." We have helped one another discover how to imagine the appropriate cultural scenario needed in order to understand and properly interpret the people and their behaviors described in the Bible.

Even as I began that project on the Gospels, I also intended to write a similar series of cultural reflections on the second or middle readings of the three-year lectionary cycle for Sundays. The middle reading was intended by the architects of the lectionary to be independent of the other two readings. The aim was to offer a semicontinuous reading from the letters attributed to Paul (and James in Year B, Twenty-Second to Twenty-Sixth Sundays in Ordinary Time). First Corinthians was spread over three years, Hebrews was spread over two years (B and C), while the other letters were completed within a given year. The letters of Peter and John and selections from Revelation were assigned to the Easter and Christmas seasons (see Sloyan). Though the author of Revelation is not the apostle John but rather one who described himself as a prophet writing for fellow Jesus-prophets (Rev 1:3), and Paul the apostle also casts himself in the role of a prophet (Gal 1:15; compare Jer 1:4), the title of this present book is *The Cultural World of the Apostles*. It treats the second or middle readings for all the Sundays and some of the feasts in Liturgical Year A.

The notion of a semicontinuous reading makes good sense. Scholars agree that in order to appreciate what a sacred author wanted to communicate, it is advisable to read that author's book or letter from beginning to end at one sitting. Given the time constraints of the liturgy, and the limited number of Sundays in a year, only parts of a letter or document are read, not the entire document. However, the architects of the lectionary did not explain why they arranged these "edited" documents in the order we find in the lectionary over the three years, or even in any given year. That order is certainly not chronological. Therefore, to help the reader understand a given document within the life-setting of its author, I give a brief indication of the probable date of that letter and some indication of the circumstances in which it was written or to which it was directed.

The principle that guided the architects of the lectionary in selecting these middle readings in the Sunday Lectionary was that they be "short and readily grasped by the people." The readings are indeed short, deliberately edited for that purpose. In many instances, however, that brevity has deprived the reader or listener of sufficient context to interpret the text-segment in a responsible way. The reading is invariably torn from its integral literary form in the letter, and sometimes verses are omitted in order to combine what remains into a reading "readily grasped by the people." As many commentators have noted, this process has unwittingly created a new scripture. These high-context documents are now raised to an even higher context! I try to present, as briefly as possible, this broader literary context for each reading as needed. (See, for example, Twenty-Seventh Sunday in Ordinary Time.)

That the architects actually believed a brief reading could be "readily grasped by the people" is astonishing. Everyone can understand the brief English sentence: "He hit it." But without the proper context, it is entirely impossible to *interpret* this sentence. Who is he? What is it? What is the meaning of "hit"? Many of the brief readings in the lectionary contain but two verses! Try to interpret 1 Corinthians 1:1-3, the reading for the Second Sunday in Ordinary Time. Then read the reflection in this book. Does your interpretation correlate with the reflection in this book? What was missing? What didn't you know about this sacred author and his community that would make a difference in your interpretation? What kind of consequences would that have for the application of these verses that you would like to make in your life, or the life of the Church?

The architects also appear to have been totally unaware of the radically different cultural settings in which the majority of contemporary readers or listeners receive these text-segments which originated in first-century Mediterranean cultural settings. That culture is the essential context for interpreting what the sacred author intended and meant. Only when the reader or listener has grasped that meaning can the reader or listener begin to make an application to his or her own cultural context. Thus, consider the selection from Philippians 4:12-14, 19-20 assigned for the Twenty-Eighth Sunday in Ordinary Time. Without an understanding of the meaning of gratitude and indebtedness in the ancient Mediterranean world, the meaning of this passage (reshaped by the architects of the lectionary!) is completely opaque for the contemporary reader. Once these key ideas are included in the interpretation, a reader can begin to explore possible adaptations of the message for readers in a very different cultural context.

Just as in my volumes on *The Cultural World of Jesus*, so too here do I use the historical critical method supplemented by insights from cultural anthropology. One understanding of history is that things were not always the way they are now. Even in antiquity, if a reader can place Paul and his letters in chronological context, it becomes easier to notice where Paul's thinking has developed or where Paul has changed his mind. Moreover, of the letters attributed to Paul in the New Testament, scholars agree that seven are indisputably authentic: 1 Thessalonians, Galatians, 1–2 Corinthians, Philemon, Romans, and Philippians. Because the authenticity of the others is disputed, they are called the Deutero-Paulines: 2 Thessalonians, Colossians, Ephesians, 1–2 Timothy, and Titus. Hebrews is not really a letter (actually, neither is Ephesians), and scholars agree that it was not written by Paul. I indicate this kind of historical information in this book at the first verses drawn from a given document of the New Testament in the lectionary. The reader is thus encouraged to consider how far removed this text-segment may be from the time of Jesus' death, from the time of the activity of his disciples, and even from the time of the reputed author. What has developed during thirty or more years? In the case of letters written by Paul's disciples in his name (e.g., 1–2 Tim, Titus), what developments have emerged?

With due respect to the architects of the lectionary, Paul cannot be "readily grasped by the people" if those people do not share his Mediterranean cultural heritage (see Malina and Neyrey). True to his own cultural heritage, Paul is a non-introspective person who thinks as he speaks. His letters record what flowed from his mouth after a fashion we might identify as stream of consciousness. Mediterranean persons often speak while they think. They do not routinely think before speaking. Hence Paul's letters often seem illogical, contradictory, and very difficult to understand. Practically all commentators admit this.

To complicate matters, in his letters (and those of other apostles) we have only half the conversation. We do not know the statements or ideas or behaviors to which he is reacting. We have only his (accurate? or biased?) report and his interpretation of what others have said or done. The experience is similar to hearing only one side of a telephone conversation. Relying upon expert Pauline scholars such as Jerome Murphy-O'Connor or Joseph Fitzmyer, I have tried to indicate where Paul or another apostle may have been quoting an opponent. This is not always evident in the text of the lectionary or the Bible.

The Mediterranean cultural information I seek to share in these reflections is not generally available in the vast majority of commentaries or homiletic aids currently on the market. The resources and scholars upon whom I have relied are listed at the end of this volume. The information provided in traditional commentaries and homiletic aids is good and presupposed by my reflections. At the same time, cultural insights may require that a reader modify that information in reaching a final interpretation of each text-segment that will respect its original cultural setting.

At the conclusion of the reflections in *The Cultural World of Jesus*, I attempted to craft a question or thought about possible relevance or challenge to the contemporary believer in his or her culture. In this volume, I have attempted the same and something more. Though the second reading was never intended by the architects of the lectionary to be related to the gospel, nearly all the preaching I have heard in all denominations that use this or a similar lectionary attempts to relate all three readings to each other (for better or for worse!). Moreover, participants in RCIA (Rite of Christian Initiation of Adults) programs who have found my previous three volumes very helpful will probably want to relate their thoughts on the second reading with the gospel. For this reason, I have attempted to suggest such a relationship where it seems possible. Readers who use this book in line with the intention of the architects of the lectionary who never intended these readings to be related to the gospel can simply ignore the final sentence or paragraph in which I do that.

My prayer is that this volume, like its predecessors and companion *(The Cultural World of Jesus; The Cultural Dictionary of the Bible)*, might contribute to an ever deeper understanding of and appreciation for our Mediterranean ancestors in the faith.

Feast of St. Clare of Assisi   John J. Pilch
August 11, 2000   Georgetown University

First Sunday of Advent
Romans 13:11-14

[For introductory comments see Fourth Sunday of Advent.] The opening phrase of today's reading, "Brothers and sisters," is repeated throughout the lectionary as an introduction to readings from various epistles. Paul never used this phrase in any of his letters. For the most part he specifically addresses "brothers." Only five times does he address or refer to a "sister" (1 Cor 7:15; 9:5; Phil 2; Rom 16:1, 15 = an actual relative of the man mentioned). The architects of the lectionary use this phrase to direct the reading to listeners in modern, Western cultures where men and women routinely mingle in the majority of public spaces. In the rigidly gender-divided Mediterranean cultures in which Paul lived and preached, it is difficult to imagine a scenario where men and women would mingle like this in a public place or worshiping congregation. When Jesus fed the crowds of four and five thousand (Mark 6:30ff. and par. and Mark 8:1-10 // Matt 15:32-39), they very likely sat down in gender-divided groups as the culture requires. Orthodox Jewish synagogues still retain a dividing boundary between men and women, and Bedouin tents have a curtain that serves the same purpose. The modern adaptation is understandable and welcome, but it should not cause listeners or readers to lose sight of the gender-based divisions that permeated the world of our ancestors in the faith.

In this passage, Paul exhorts believers to behave properly, that is, with a concern for true honor. The language of day/night, light/darkness symbolizes good and evil and reflects honor and shame. Believers must behave honorably all the time but now is an especially appropriate time *(kairos)*. The six shameful lifestyles he specifies (v. 13) reflect the three zones of the human body (heart-eyes; mouth-ears; hands-feet) which carry consistent symbolic meaning throughout the Bible (emotion fused thought; self-expressive speech; purposeful behavior or activity). When all zones are in harmony, the person is whole, healthy, holy, pure. When any zone is out of harmony, that person needs conversion or healing.

Eating and drinking excesses (orgies and drunkenness) reflect the zone of mouth-ears, usually self-expressive speech or communication. Sexual excess and lust (promiscuity and licentiousness) reflect two zones: heart-eyes, symbolizing emotion guided-thought by which a person decides to behave in this shameful way, and hands-feet, symbolizing purposeful activity in the very means by which one puts thought into action. Rivalry and jealousy also reflect two zones: mouth-ears and heart-eyes. Paul's point is that believers should avoid completely and entirely every conceivable shameful human behavior but strive instead to maintain a completely comprehensive honorable lifestyle. One should not yield to unredeemed and misdirected living (this is what Paul means by "flesh"), but should rather imitate the quality and direction of the life of Jesus ("put on the Lord Jesus Christ," v. 14).

The notion of "awaking from sleep" (Rom 13:11) and "staying awake" (Matt 24:42) links this reading with the gospel. Both readings challenge the modern believer to examine one's lifestyle and evaluate one's personal level of preparation. Are you prepared?

Second Sunday of Advent
Romans 15:4-9

Nowhere in this letter does Paul mention "Romans," even though this word with its potential for misunderstanding the identity of the recipients has been enshrined in the traditional title: "to the Romans." Paul wrote this letter mainly for fellow Judeans living in Rome. In chapters 14 and 15, he describes two factions in that Judean community: those who are "strong in faith" and those who are "weak in faith." Scholars are not agreed whether this reflects an actual situation or is rather a presentation of ideal-types.

Whatever one decides, some basic values that dominate Mediterranean cultures help create an appropriate scenario for reading these verses. Keep in mind that kinship and politics are the two principal free-standing social institutions of this culture. Paul's extensive use of the term "brother" (and "sister") indicates that his major concern is domestic religion rather than political religion ("temple"). Judeans who have embraced Jesus as Messiah form a surrogate family or fictive kinship group. In many cases, a family ejected from their midst those members who accepted this crucified Jesus as Messiah. Further, Mediterranean beliefs concerning family are exemplified in this Mediterranean saying: "I against my brother. I and my brother against our cousin. I, my brother, and my cousin against other families," and so on. Thus, a second cultural value becomes apparent. Mediterranean cultures, in general, are agonistic. They hold strong opinions, enjoy conflict, and are ever ready to argue. Conflict is dangerous because it can escalate to violence, then to the shedding of blood which results in blood-feud for generations. Since no one really desires this, a mediator is a key figure for maintaining family solidarity and harmony between and among families (see Matt 5:9 more appropriately translated: "Blessed are the mediators, for they shall be called children of God").

In this segment of his letter, Paul plays the role of such a mediator exhorting his fellow Judeans living in Rome to forego dissension and conflict. They should curb their inclination to argue and disagree. Rather they should "think in harmony with one another" so that "with one accord" they might "with one voice" truly honor God the father of our Lord, Jesus Messiah.

Jesus ministered to his own compatriots to demonstrate God's loyalty to the promises made to the Patriarchs, which in turn their descendants can also trust. This is God's mercy, which in Mediterranean terms means being faithful to meeting one's interpersonal obligations. When others, especially non-Judeans, witness such loyalty and mercy they will honor and respect a God who behaves in this way.

Today's gospel (Matt 3:1-12) echoes similar convictions about how God could demonstrate fidelity to the patriarch Abraham in a worst-case scenario (v. 9). The Baptist's rebuke to the Pharisees and Sadducees for not taking proper action (vv. 8, 10) is similar to Paul's claim that both weak and strong in faith might be missing the point. How might contemporary believers achieve the ability to "think in harmony with one another" that Paul urges?

Third Sunday of Advent
James 5:7-10

Tradition has identified this James as "the brother of the Lord" (Gal 1:19; Matt 13:44; Mark 6:3), also known as James of Jerusalem and James the Just. Contemporary scholarly research has concluded that the author of this letter is very likely a Messianist (that is, someone who accepted Jesus as Messiah, or in modern terms: a Christian) who was familiar with Hellenism and Judaism. Following a common practice in antiquity, he wrote under the name of James in the latter part of the first century A.D.

Rev. Dr. John H. Elliott (1993) of the University of San Francisco identified the letter's major theme as concern for the completeness and wholeness of the readers, their community, and their relationship to God (Jas 1:2-4). The body of the letter (Jas 1:13–5:12) contains seven exhortations, each of which contrasts negative indictments of unwholeness (divided or divisive attitudes and behaviors) with positive recommendations for integrity and wholeness.

Section 6, from which today's reading is drawn, criticizes arrogant planning and boasting (4:13-17) and oppression of laborers and the just by the rich (5:1-6). This is the negative section. In the positive section (5:7-11), the author urges the recipients (and readers/listeners) of this letter to wait patiently for the Lord's coming and to remain steadfast.

The original recipients of this letter lived outside Palestine and represented a mixture of cultural backgrounds and social strata (rich and poor, teachers, elders, and just ordinary folk).

Obviously, this produced a plurality of viewpoints and norms for social behavior, tensions between rich and poor, strife and division, and more. Those who suffered irremediably lost patience and hope. Some even defected from the community.

Section 6 concerns the neglect, exploitation, and oppression of the poor by the wealthy who cheated their laborers, stockpiled harvests for conspicuous consumption, and even killed the righteous. It is important to keep this scenario in mind as one seeks to understand today's verses, carved from their fuller context.

Some motifs stand out: an exhortation to patience (vv. 7, 8, 10), the imminent coming of the Lord (vv. 7, 8) who will also judge (v. 9). If, as suspected, this letter was written in Jerusalem before the year A.D. 70, the air was rife with hints of imminent cataclysm. If it was written afterward, the destruction of the Temple would give different meaning to the concept and objects of judgment. Nevertheless, it is not difficult to appreciate an atmosphere of frustration and desperation these verses and their context evoke.

The author offers two models to imitate: the Palestinian farmer who must patiently await early and late rains (see Pilch 1999: 178–84, "weather"), and the prophets who suffered unjustly. Matthew (5:12 and 23:29-39; see also Acts 7:52) reflects the belief of early Messianists that their persecution and suffering is simply an extension and continuation of that of the prophets.

The link of this reading to the gospel (Matt 11:2-11) is quite likely the idea of a prophet who suffers (the Baptist is in prison) and feels frustrated ("Are you the one . . ., or should we look for another?" Matt 11:3). How often do modern believers wonder: "Is this leader (or solution) the one, or ought we look for another?" "What should we do?" "Shall we continue to search?"

Fourth Sunday of Advent
Romans 1:1-7

How would one write a letter to people the majority of whom one hasn't personally met? That is Paul's challenge in this letter, written around A.D. 57–58, from Corinth or Cenchrae, its port. According to the formula that was common in antiquity, each letter began with the statement: "A [is sending this] to B." Here, Paul (alone) sends this letter to "all the beloved of God in Rome." Nowhere does the letter mention "Romans." These "beloved of God" are fellow-Judeans. Only occasionally does Paul refer specifically to non-Judeans (e.g., Rom 11:13).

Paul presents himself from three perspectives: *slave* of Messiah Jesus, called to be an *apostle,* and *set apart* for the Gospel. The ancients did not know freedom as we know it. The majority had to serve or be slave to someone. Believers freed by God from slavery to sin ought now to "render slave service" (literal translation of Gal 5:13) to one another. This explains why Paul likes to describe himself as slave (1 Cor 9:29) or servant (2 Corinthians 5) for the sake of Jesus.

Perhaps Paul's favorite self-description is apostle, someone called and commissioned by God with full power to fulfill a very specific task. This aspect of his identity was often challenged, but Paul always defended it resolutely and decisively (e.g., Gal 1:1-2, 11-12, 15-17, etc.). This identity places Paul in a line continuous with such as Abraham, Moses, Joshua, Jeremiah, and others.

Third, Paul is convinced he has been set apart by God, even before birth, like Jeremiah (1:5) or the Servant of God (Isa 49:1) for this role of proclaiming God's good news. The message is about Jesus raised from the dead and thereby established as Son of God in power requiring loyal obedience from those who embrace him.

Paul did not create this identity while writing this letter. It was the result of an intense experience of God in an altered state of consciousness (Gal 1:12; even Luke agrees in the version of this event that he reports in Acts 9; 22; 26) much earlier in his life. The result of this experience was Paul's unshakable confidence in his ministry and a determination to fulfill it no matter what the costs.

In today's gospel (Matt 1:18-24), Joseph knows he is not the father of the child in Mary's womb and must make some serious decisions. Divine communication in a dream gives him confidence similar to Paul's regarding what must be done. How does a modern believer living in a culture which suspects such experiences (trances and dreams) gain the assurance and confidence available to Paul and Joseph that helped them to live their faith boldly?

Vigil of the Nativity
Acts 13:16-17, 22-25

Scholars agree that this "sermon" preached by Paul is in reality a Lukan composition following the pattern of earlier sermons (Acts 2:38-40; 3:19-26). Typically there are three parts: God's promise in history (vv. 16-25), the Jesus kerygma as fulfillment of the promise (vv. 26-37), and an exhortation to faith and forgiveness (vv. 38-41). Today's verses present a selective summary of history. God chose our ancestors, among whom was David, "a man after my own [God's] heart." Jesus, heralded by John, was David's descendant and savior of Israel.

What does it mean to be a person "after God's own heart"? Everything human beings know and say about God is based on human experience. In theological jargon, "all theology is analogy." Further, human experience is culturally shaped. Our non-introspective (actually, anti-introspective!) Mediterranean ancestors in the faith viewed human beings externally as composed of three interacting zones of the body: heart-eyes, mouth-ears, and hands-feet. Heart-eyes symbolized emotion-fused thought, mouth-ears self-expressive speech, and hands-feet purposeful action.

In the New Testament, God too functions in terms of these three zones. Relative to Jesus as son, the Father functions in terms of the heart-eyes zone: God "*sees* in secret" (Matt 6:18), *knows* our hearts (Luke 16:15), *loves* the world (John 3:16), *judges* each according to his deeds (1 Pet 1:17), and so on. Relative to God, Jesus as Word functions in terms of the mouth-ears zone: he reveals the Father (John 1:1ff.). The Father *has spoken* to us by a Son (Heb 1:12). In other words, Jesus is the mouth-ears of God. The hands-feet zone applied to the Father invariably refers to the Spirit who exhibits power, activity, doing, and effectiveness. The "hand [or spirit] of the Lord was upon" many of the prophets (1 Kgs 18:46; 2 Kgs 3:15; etc.). This typical Mediterranean way of viewing the human person may well be the source of the later Christian development of the notion of the Trinity.

Thus, a person "after God's own heart" is one who relates harmoniously with the divine intellect, will, judgment, conscience, personality thrust, core personality—to borrow words from Western cultural perspectives. Such a person is totally pleasing to God. The speech that Luke crafts for Paul draws this phrase from 1 Sam 13:14 where Samuel tells Saul that God has rejected him as king in favor of David. Saul tended to overstep his authority. Too often he took matters into his own hands rather than obey God's law strictly (1 Sam 13:1-15, esp. v. 14; 15:10-33, esp. vv. 11 and 19). David was one who would "carry out my [God's] every wish." The gospel for this vigil (Matt 1:18-25) describes the circumstances of the birth of Jesus, one who carried out "God's every wish" even more faithfully than David. In David and Jesus modern believers face a powerful challenge to become people after God's own heart. How do we believers accomplish that?

Nativity: Midnight Mass
Titus 2:11-14

This letter (along with 1 and 2 Timothy) has been dubbed by tradition as one of the Pastoral epistles. They have been called Pastoral epistles since the eighteenth century because they are addressed to "pastors" of early communities. For this reason, the anonymous person who wrote this letter under the name of Paul, who was already dead, is usually called "the Pastor."

The architects of the lectionary have omitted the first and very important word in today's reading: "for." In Greek this particle always points backward. The verses that follow this word provide the motive for what preceded (vv. 1-10 are guidelines for behavior based on age and gender: older men/older women; younger men/younger women). Thus have the architects made these verses somewhat "free floating" in the liturgy.

The key word now is "appeared" (v. 11), and its tense in Greek signals a once-and-for-always perspective. How has the grace of God appeared once-and-for-always? The noun "appearance" occurs just six times in the New Testament and always in reference to Jesus. So the process by which God relates to humans (= "grace") has been revealed once and forever in Jesus, in what he said and did and means for us (= salvation).

What is God doing for us? "Training us"; that is, forming us as authentic human beings in all respects: emotionally, intellectually, socially, religiously, politically, and any other way we might imagine. In modern terms, God is relating to us now holistically.

How does God train us? We must reject (a) godless ways and (b) worldly desires. Instead, on the positive side we must live (b') temperately, justly, and (a') devoutly. Notice the arrangement of ideas, so common in the Bible (a, b, b', a'). Godless ways would be equivalent to religious indifferentism or atheistic secularism. If science or some other idol usurps God's role to be in charge of life, the result is a godless way of life.

Worldly desires might be interpreted as accepting the dictates of one's culture without critical evaluation. Many people in Western culture derive a sense of self-worth from having a job or the right kind of job. Does human worth and identity depend on a job, or on something other than one's job? Instead, believers are called to lead sensible, self-controlled lives and to live justly or uprightly. This means one must live in good interpersonal relationships with other human beings. Finally, to live devoutly is to acknowledge God's reign in our personal lives. While this may sound like excessive reliance upon personal efforts, the Pastor says exactly the opposite: it is God's grace that makes good living possible. God's activity on our behalf through Jesus makes us true human beings. Moreover, God's training is effective because of Jesus' voluntary death in total obedience to the Father so that we might be cleansed and eager to do good.

This reflection on the consequences of Jesus' life and death for us is a fitting transition to the gospel (Luke 2:1-14) which announces the birth of Jesus. Clearly the feast is about much more than the joy, lights, and gifts so characteristic of the season.

Nativity: Mass at Dawn
Titus 3:4-7

Scholars recognize these verses as a popular "creed" which the Pastor inserted at this point in his letter as a comment on good deeds (3:1, 5, 8) and bad deeds (3:9). (Examples of other such creedal statements in the Pastorals would be 1 Tim 1:15; 2:4-6; 3:16; 6:12-16; 2 Tim 1:8-10; Titus 2:11-14.) Such creedal statements may have originated in the context of liturgies. If so, the Pastor's ready reliance on creeds in his instructions about proper behavior (good and bad deeds) is an excellent example of moving from liturgy to life among our ancestors in the faith.

The Pastor's creed-based observation is that good deeds by themselves don't merit anything from God (v. 5). Rather, everything is a free gift coming to us through baptism. But remember that in Mediterranean culture, there really are no free gifts. Every gift expects that a gift will be given in return, or at least some response will be made. In the present context, the response is "good deeds."

Once again, these verses seem well suited to the gospel (Luke 2:15-20) in which the shepherds who received word of the birth of Jesus don't just put it on their calendars or on their lists of things "to do." Rather, they immediately (so typical of the Mediterranean culture's intense focus on the present) go to Bethlehem, see for themselves, and return glorifying and praising God. Would you consider yourself a person who acts promptly on a resolution or one who procrastinates? Would it make a difference?

Nativity: Mass during the Day
Hebrews 1:1-6

Writing in the name of Paul sometime between A.D. 60 and 100, this anonymous author has produced a masterpiece of literature and theological reflection about Jesus. These opening verses sum up the essay and the significance of today's feast: Jesus is Son and word of God, God's definitive self-disclosure. These verses are also very different in form and content from the customary opening verses of Paul's letters.

The final verses (4-6) emphasize that Jesus is superior to the angels. Indeed he is an agent of revelation far superior to the angels. (For angels as agents or mediators of revelation see 1 Kgs 13:18; Isaiah 6; Daniel 7–12; 2 Esdras 3–14.) Since the author does not engage in specific polemics, scholars have been unable to determine the reason for this emphasis upon Jesus as superior to the angels. Some scholars think this community may have been attracted to or participated in worshiping angels. The letter provides no evidence for this hypothesis. What is more likely is that the community may have thought they were worshiping with angels (e.g., Isa 6:3). This is a familiar idea in first-century Judaism which later became an element of Christian liturgical practice. Variations on the phrase "And so, with all the choirs of angels in heaven we proclaim your glory" appear in prefaces throughout the Liturgical Year. If the author thought that associating Jesus with the angels in some way minimized Jesus' role as mediator, it is surprising that he does not dwell upon it more explicitly.

14

The author's purpose is clear. He seeks to reinforce the sublime dimension of Jesus' exalted status which guarantees salvation to believers. This strong statement prepares the way for his subsequent presentation of Jesus' humiliation which gained that salvation for his followers.

This reading links well with the gospel (John 1:1-18), which is the classic statement of Jesus' exalted status in the New Testament. It also looks back to the gospel for the Mass at Dawn, which highlighted a special function for angels at the birth of Jesus. Given the popularity of angels in the contemporary world, Hebrews invite modern believers to examine their faith and make certain that Jesus remains central and unsurpassed as our mediator with the Father.

Sunday within the Octave of Christmas: Holy Family Sunday
Colossians 3:12-21

Modern scholars are divided about the authenticity of this letter. Until the nineteenth century, the traditional view was that Paul wrote it. Closer examination of the letter surfaced significant differences with the authentic Pauline letters leading scholars to say it was likely written between A.D. 70 and 80 by someone who knew the Pauline tradition very well. Today's verses form part of the customary, hortatory conclusion in Paul's letters.

Specifically, vv. 12-17 (shorter reading for today) present a list of virtues for emulation while vv. 12-21 (longer reading) are part of a household code. Other examples of virtue-lists are Gal 5:22-23; Phil 4:8; Eph 4:2-3; 1 Tim 4:12; 6:11; 2 Tim 2:22; 3:10; 1 Pet 3:8; 2 Pet 1:5-7. Such lists were very common in paganism and usually centered around the four cardinal virtues or the eight parts of the soul identified by the Stoics: the five senses, the faculty of speech, the intellectual faculty which is the mind itself, and the generative faculty (Diogenes Laertius: *Vit.* 7:110). In Paul and his tradition, such lists are very rare and appear mostly in the Deutero-Paulines (letters presumed not to have been written by Paul). But more importantly, as is evident in this passage, the focus in the New Testament is love *(agape)* and its very obvious expressions: forgiveness, goodness, and mercy. To these the author of Colossians adds heartfelt compassion, kindness, humility, gentleness, and patience following the Lord's example.

Household codes, or more broadly speaking social codes, govern specific social relationships. This is a general type of exhortation and instruction that was very popular in Hellenistic philosophy. Such codes list the obligations or duties of members of Messianist households: husbands and wives; parents and children; and masters and slaves. Other New Testament examples include: Eph 5:22–6:9; 1 Pet 1:13–3:7; Titus 2:1-10; 1 Tim 2:8-15; 6:1-2). One feature of these codes is a phrase which troubles many contemporary believers: "be subordinate [or subject] to." Paul's exhortation "Let every person be subordinate to the higher authorities" (Rom 13:1) found a variety of responses ranging from martyrdom (Acts 7:57-60), to appeal to Caesar (Acts 25:11), or to the axiom that we ought obey God rather than civil authority (Acts 5:29).

The exhortation to "be subordinate" applies to all Christians according to their cultural situation. In Paul's patriarchal culture, it was important to maintain the authority of the patriarch lest society disintegrate. The probable reason for his exhortations to the family (household codes) was "enthusiasm," especially one that would deny social roles and the concrete conditions of political, social, and kinship or family-like settings. "Enthusiasts" were Messianists (believers in Jesus) who emphasized the "freedom *from*" obtained by the death and resurrection of Jesus (e.g., Gal 3:26-28), but set aside the "freedom *for*" *serving* others in the here and now world (Gal 5:13-15). Paul's concern was his social context. It was not to establish a normative "Christian" social structure for generations to come. For the Pauline tradition, the only way Jesus is Lord in the here and now is by the word of preaching (kerygma) and the servanthood of the community. Anything that thwarts these is enthusiastic and has no solid basis in the tradition.

This selection relates well to the gospel (Matt 2:13-15, 19-23) which recounts how Joseph took care of his family which did not hold a family conference to discern whether Joseph's plan had merit or Mary might have had a better idea. Contemporary Western family structures are quite different from those of the ancient Middle East. We admire and appreciate the latter but must work out our own structures based on the pattern of the quality and direction of the life of Jesus.

January 1:
Octave Day of Christmas:
Solemnity of the Blessed Virgin Mary, The Mother of God
Galatians 4:4-7

[Paul wrote this letter from Ephesus in a very angry mood around 54 A.D.] For Paul, the advent of Jesus marked the beginning of a new "time." Specifically, it was the redemptive death of Jesus that formed the dividing line signaling the end of one age and the beginning of another (then–now; once–but now). Jesus was born an Israelite and circumcised, hence he became subject to the law (then). But his death abrogated the covenant of law and established a new covenant of faith and grace (now; Gal 3:13-14). In his own life, Jesus manifests the precise pattern of the covenant of faith, its significance, and how it works in day-to-day life. Jesus is the unique "son" that God promised to Abraham (Gal 3:16), thus becoming a model for whoever would be son (or daughter) with God (Gal 4:5-7). This defines the status of any and every believer. Just as Jesus prayed to his Abba (Mark 14:36, the only place this word appears in the Gospels), so his followers are filled with the Spirit and pray as he did: "Abba, Father" (Gal 4:6).

It is probably unnecessary but still helpful to remind ourselves that the Aramaic word "Abba" never meant "Daddy," but rather exactly as reported in the Greek of Mark meant and was understood as "Father." Even in the English language, there is a difference between "Father" and "Daddy." In 1988, James Barr reviewed the linguistic evidence and noted that in its cultural context, that is, the ancient Israelite social system, Abba was a term of formal address. It was not used as a familiar, intimate, warm, and loving term (see Pilch 1999: 1–3). The significance for these passages (Mark and Galatians) is that now after the death of Jesus, his followers have the same relationship to God that Jesus had. God is Father to believers. That is indeed good news. The term, however, fits well into the Mediterranean cultural matrix where love for the father is always demonstrated in a respectful way. In this culture, the son is not the father's equal or "pal." As reflected in Sirach (3:6-7), the culture notes that "he who fears the LORD honors his father, / and serves his parents as rulers."

Luke (2:16-21) depicts the way in which Jesus was indeed subject to his parents from the very beginning. He was circumcised on the eighth day and given the name assigned by the angel. The pattern of his life lived faithfully under the law helps to appreciate the new relationship with God that Jesus made possible for all, Israelite and non-Israelite alike.

Second Sunday after Christmas
Ephesians 1:3-6, 15-18

Contemporary scholarly opinion lists this letter among the Deutero-Paulines, that is, it was likely written after Paul's death by disciples sometime between A.D. 80 and 100. These verses from a letter in the Pauline tradition are part of the customary blessing (vv. 3-14) and thanksgiving (vv. 15-23) sections which begin most of the letters. Why should we bless God? Primarily because God chose us in Jesus just as he chose special people before us (see Deut 14:2). Given the gratuitous nature of God's choice, one can only marvel and be grateful. Of course, that election involves an obligation: God's chosen people must be holy and without blemish in God's presence. Yet another reason for requiring such holiness and purity is that the Ephesian congregation, like the Colossian congregation, was convinced that angels were in the midst of the worshiping community (see Eph 3:10; also 2:6). This is similar to the sentiments at Qumran where anyone physically blemished "shall not enter to take their place among the congregation of famous men, for the angels of holiness are among their congregation" (1QSa 2:8-9).

God has not just chosen us but also adopted us. Scholars observe that in this culture where family (kinship) is one of the dominant social institutions and is rather extensive and complex, there was no mechanism for adoption. That Paul can conclude that God adopted us is an interesting breakthrough. Those who heard this from Paul and his circle would be awed. God's election bestows incredible honor and far-reaching consequences.

The thanksgiving section (vv. 15-18) appears to have been patterned after Phlm 4-5. Paul prays that they may receive wisdom and revelation so that they may come to know God even better. Wisdom in the Bible involves practical or experiential knowledge and the ability to choose proper conduct. In Paul, wisdom often involved understanding more clearly God's activity in Jesus and the benefits believers receive from such knowledge. The upshot of Paul's prayer is that the Ephesians might appreciate the immense privileges that God has bestowed upon them.

The gospel for today (John 1:1-18) talks about the Word who, literally in Greek, "pitched his tent among us" (v. 14). Those who received him were empowered to become "children of God" (v. 12). The Ephesian verses provide still further information about the truly blessed condition of being adopted by God. No doubt all modern believers can readily repeat Paul's prayer that they, too, might understand and appreciate the incredible honor of being so chosen by God. How amazing is this God!

January 6: Epiphany
Ephesians 3:2-3a, 5-6

The author of Ephesians (not Paul, but a disciple writing between 80–100 A.D.) repeats Paul's great insight here, that non-Israelites (Gentiles) have full and co-equal membership with Israelites in the Church through Christ Jesus. In the Greek texts three adjectives with the prefix syn- (together) make this point emphatically (co-heirs, co-members, co-partners, v. 6). Actually, the insight results from a direct revelation from God (compare Gal 1:12, 16) which by this time in the tradition has become normative. Given the history of the chosen people, the covenant, and related concepts, only God could have revealed that the divine will now include non-Israelites in that people. This idea would be too preposterous for any human being to initiate on personal initiative.

Another interesting point is that this revelation/insight has been given to "holy apostles and prophets" (v. 5). Scholars remind us that Paul (e.g., in Galatians 1–2) insisted that he alone received the distinctive revelation concerning the place of non-Israelites in the Church. That the author of Ephesians now extends it to others (apostles and prophets) is a strong argument that this is an author writing in the name of Paul, and not Paul himself.

The common link between this reading and the gospel for today's feast (Matt 2:1-12) is the Magi, non-Israelites who come to do homage to Jesus at his birth. In Romans, Paul makes the boldest statement of his understanding of the relationship of non-Israelites to Israelites by calling the grafting of non-Israelites to Israelites "unnatural" or "contrary to nature" (Rom 11:24). Only a revelation from God could convince humans that this is the divine will. Contemporary Church members who are overwhelmingly of non-Israelite lineage should be awed by God's decision. Today's feast provides an opportunity to formulate a convincing reply to a question frequently asked by outsiders: "Knowing the history of the Church and its warts, why do you remain a Christian?"

Baptism of the Lord
(First Sunday in Ordinary Time)
Acts 10:34-38

Scholars recognize that Luke has created all the speeches in
Acts to help him present his view of an early community of
believers. Peter's speech here in Acts 10, delivered in a non-
Israelite (Gentile) setting, represents Luke's attempt to le-
gitimize the place of non-Israelite god-fearers in the Church
and to soft-pedal the marginalization they experienced in
Jerusalem. Such were excluded from offering sacrifice in the
Temple. Cornelius, a non-Israelite god-fearer, received instructions to contact Peter in a vision that occurred at the
ninth hour, the time for the evening sacrifice in the Temple.
Moreover, the angel assures him: "Your prayers and alms-
giving have ascended as a memorial offering before God"
(Acts 10:4). Phrases similar to "ascend as a memorial offering" appear in the Greek Bible (LXX) relative to the fragrance
of sacrifices arising to YHWH in the Temple. In other words,
Luke is saying that Cornelius' alms and sacrifice which he
was not allowed to offer in the Temple are quite acceptable
to God. Indeed, these are equivalent to what an Israelite
would offer in the Temple.

Peter describes God's behavior in this matter by drawing
upon the core-cultural value of honor. Literally, he says that
God does not "lift the face" only of certain people (v. 34).
Honor claims in the Mediterranean world depend upon public

approval by others who decide whether the claims are valid or spurious. God does not behave like that. God is not deceived but can read hearts (Acts 15:8; compare 1 Sam 16:7) and recognize legitimate claims to honor. Thus any one in any ethnic group (v. 35) who respects (= fears) God and acts uprightly is pleasing to God. Cornelius behaves in this way and is thereby acceptable to God.

Finally, notice the theocentric focus of these verses. The topic is God's saving action through Jesus and his apostolic witnesses on behalf of the Israelites and every nation. Jesus mediates God's plan of redemption in his ministry, death, and resurrection, which was subsequently proclaimed by divinely appointed eyewitnesses.

One motif that joins these verses with the gospel for today's feast (Matt 3:13-17) is the question of who is pleasing to God. The voice from the sky at Jesus' baptism identifies him as pleasing to God (Matt 3:17). Peter recognizes that Cornelius, a non-Israelite, is also pleasing to God, and Peter's statement about Jesus ends with the observation that he was able to heal "for God was with him" (Acts 10:30). How ought a modern believer behave to merit such an acknowledgment, namely, that one is pleasing to God, or that God is with that believer?

Second Sunday in Ordinary Time
1 Corinthians 1:1-3

This letter was probably written about the year A.D. 54. In the same way that he introduces himself at the beginning of most of his letters, so too in this letter Paul declares his ascribed honor: God called Paul to be an apostle of Messiah Jesus. Paul was adamant about his identity as an apostle. According to Luke (Acts 1:21-22), only those who were with Jesus from his baptism to his ascension could be apostles. Paul believed otherwise (Gal 1:1): God chose him to be an apostle.

Who is Sosthenes and why is he mentioned as a co-sender with Paul? The plurals in 1 Cor 1:18-31 and 1 Cor 2:6-16 suggest he contributed to these sections. He appears to have been familiar with the factions in the Corinthian community. It is therefore plausible but not certain that this is the same Sosthenes who was president of the synagogue in Corinth and who was beaten up when Gallio dismissed Judean charges against Paul (Acts 18:17). The beating might have occurred because Sosthenes had become a believer in Jesus. Murphy-O'Connor discerns that Sosthenes might have been an insightful conversationalist but unable to communicate simply and clearly in writing. Paul seems disappointed in his contributions, for he follows each of the cooperatively written sections with a statement of his own position (2:1-5; 3:1-4). That the plurals don't appear afterward suggest Paul dropped him as a collaborator.

The addressees, the community of believers in Corinth, are reminded of their ascribed honor as well: they have been sanctified in Messiah Jesus and called (by God) to be holy (or called to be "saints"). The word "sanctified" or "made holy" means to be set apart for God and dedicated to serving God with awe and respect. Believers in Corinth must meet this challenge and strive to be worthy of their call.

Then Paul adds an interesting note: they are called to be holy "with all those everywhere who call upon the name of the Lord" (v. 2). This is a not-so-subtle way of saying: "you are not the only believers on the face of the earth." Paul uses these introductory comments to lay a foundation for the scolding he will begin in v. 10 for the shameful divisions in this community. Splintering into factions is scandalous and shameful (1 Cor 11:16).

The motivating power of a concern for honor is probably lost on Western readers, but Paul's Mediterranean readers/ listeners would be very much affected by this. Paul is touching the central value in their life.

Today's gospel (John 1:29-34) reports John's statement concerning the ascribed honor of Jesus: he is no one less than the son of God. Ascribed honor is one link between the gospel and the epistle for this feast. Modern Western believers might reflect on the fact that ascribed honor does not derive from personal efforts or achievement but rather from circumstances beyond one's control like birth into an honorable family. Thus the familiar theme: the honor God grants is the only one that counts. What distinctive honor has God bestowed on Paul, the Corinthian believers, Jesus, or the modern followers of Jesus?

Third Sunday in Ordinary Time
1 Corinthians 1:10-13, 17

Paul's image of the Church as the Body of Christ is familiar (1 Cor 6:15; 12:12). Just as physical integrity is a mark of the wholeness or purity of the physical body, so too is communal unity the mark of holiness or purity of the social body. The most dangerous threat to a whole body is mutilation or some bodily defect. The greatest threat to a holy body is divisions, factions, pollution. In today's verses, Paul laments that various groups in the Corinthian community prefer different "heads" for the social body: Paul, Apollos, Cephas, Christ.

From a cultural perspective, the problem in Corinth is not uncommon. Mediterranean cultures in general are agonistic. They are prone to conflict, argument, and outright hostility. The situation in Corinth was very likely sharpened because of rivalry among the preachers: Paul, Apollos (see e.g., Phil 1:15-18; 1 Cor 3:4; Gal 1:6-9), and Cephas. Originally from Alexandria (Acts 18:24–19:1), Apollos preached in Corinth when Paul was not present (1 Cor 3:6). He was with Paul in Ephesus when this letter was written (1 Cor 1:12). In Mediterranean culture, even friends will play the game of one-upmanship. Differences in skills and abilities play a key role. This may have been the situation between Apollos and Paul. Cephas may not have preached in Corinth, but he seems to have had a following who embraced a vision of a believer's life different from Paul's (see Galatians 2).

The Greek form of Paul's question "Is Christ divided?" expects an affirmative answer. Therefore, "Christ" in this passage means community (just as in 1 Cor 6:15; 12:12). Paul is lamenting the community's division manifested in the factions and caused—no doubt unintentionally—by the preaching. Hence Paul's concluding statement that authentic preaching ought not be rooted in clever rhetoric but rather in the meaning of Jesus' suffering in which the preacher may also have to participate.

The gospel for this Sunday (Matt 4:12-13) tells of Jesus preaching repentance and healing the people at the beginning of his ministry. This is an interesting contrast to the preaching in Corinth lamented by Paul which promoted factions and divisions. Here is a good opportunity to reflect on the effects of contemporary preaching by ordained and nonordained alike: Is it therapeutic or does it cause divisions?

Fourth Sunday in Ordinary Time
1 Corinthians 1:26-31

The preceding verses (18-25) set the context for today's reflection. They present Christ crucified, who from a cultural perspective (honor and shame) is foolishness, shameful, a stumbling block. But having raised him from the dead, God has made Jesus to symbolize the power and wisdom of God. As Isaiah remarked: "I [God] will destroy the wisdom of the wise, and the learning of the learned I will set aside" (29:14). Sometimes God is predictable, but at other times God loves reversals.

Speaking from the perspective of honor and shame, Paul reminds the Corinthian believers of God's penchant for turning things upside down. Instead of selecting honorable folk to achieve the divine purposes (the wise and strong, which would make sense in human calculation), God has selected the shameful (foolish, weak, lowly, and despised). The divine choice removes the opportunity to boast from both sides: the honorable and the shameful. Modern believers must make a strong effort to appreciate the powerful influence of honor and shame in the lives of the ancients. Still, modern believers are no less free from the powerful influences of their own culture's core values which can work for good or ill in human life.

It is also important to note Paul's focus on God in this passage. It is because of God's activity in Jesus that believers can gain true insight (wisdom) into the meaning of human life. They should seek to separate themselves from sinners (sanctification) so as to curb the controlling power of sin (redemption) and thereby become what they ought to be in God's eyes (righteous).

The corresponding Gospel (Matt 5:1-12a) presents Matthew's version of the makarisms (beatitudes) which are in reality value statements. In these statements, Jesus announces reversals of that culture's ideas of what constitutes true honor or characterizes truly honorable people. Moreover, the passive voice (e.g., will be comforted; will be satisfied; etc.) is known as the "theological or divine passive." It is the way our ancestors in the faith could talk about God without mentioning God's name. The reversals worked by God in Jesus' beatitudes are manifested in the experience of reversals by the Corinthians in their community. How have God's reversals worked to further the divine will in your life?

Fifth Sunday in Ordinary Time
1 Corinthians 2:1-5

Paul draws on yet another value in Mediterranean culture to explain the success of his preaching. In his behavior, Paul adopts a stance of "cultural humility." As these verses illustrate, he did not preach with rhetorical polish or cleverness. He deliberately avoids creating the impression that he is lording it over his audience or his rivals. In contrast, given Western culture's emphasis on achievement, it is imperative to have a résumé, a press release, or a vanity wall displaying all one's awards. Humility could be culturally harmful in the West. Paul came instead in weakness, fear, and trembling through which the power of the Spirit instilled and nourished the faith of the Corinthians.

Though he sometimes displays charismatic strength and power (Gal 3:3-5; 1 Thess 1:5; 1 Cor 14:18), Paul routinely presents himself as he does here: weak and of no account (2 Cor 10:10; Gal 4:13-14). But as he states in today's verses, appearances may be deceiving. Weakness can be strength; foolishness may be wisdom (1 Cor 1:18-25). In Paul's eyes, his sufferings, humiliations and weakness are indications of his legitimation by God and not a disqualification as some at Corinth may have thought (1 Cor 1:17; 2 Cor 4:7-11).

This distinction between appearance and reality is fundamental in Mediterranean culture, though most often appearance counts more than the reality. The impressive front one puts on may mask a very different reality. Anti-introspective

Mediterranean people can judge only by appearances (1 Sam 16:7). Of course, such judgments are often erroneous! This is Paul's point. To judge him on the basis of appearance (which he might have deliberately contrived) is to misunderstand the power of God who enjoys turning human judgments upside-down. Because his message is Christ crucified, Paul may have selected a corresponding posture (weakness) to underscore God's good pleasure with Jesus and with himself.

In today's gospel (Matt 5:13-16), Jesus speaks of salt which, though harmless in appearance, served in the ancient world to light the fire that burned the fuel (camel and donkey dung) and to sustain its flames which bring heat and light (see Pilch 1999:4–5). So, too Paul, who appears weak and powerless, manages in his preaching to serve as a channel of God's power. Who or what are the weak and powerless channels of God's power in the modern world?

Sixth Sunday in Ordinary Time
1 Corinthians 2:6-10

Yet another dimension of Mediterranean "cultural humility" is mild sarcasm or irony. Some people in Corinth considered themselves to be "mature" or "perfect" because of a special wisdom they thought they possessed but that others lacked. They considered themselves "spirit-people" *(pneumatikoi)* and looked down upon these others as "children," less enlightened, less mature, and certainly less perfect *(psychikoi)*. Paul, the weak and shameful preacher, promises to give wisdom to these mature "spirit-people," but immediately qualifies it as something they didn't expect to hear. It is God's wisdom, mysterious and hidden, implying that what these self-styled "mature" people possess is nothing of the sort.

The wisdom of God is the divine plan for salvation, the goal of which was to restore honor or glory to God's creatures who lost it in the Fall. The humiliating death of Jesus restored this honor, making him indeed the Lord of honor or glory. The spirit-people focused on this aspect of Jesus alone and chose to neglect the fact that it was the crucifixion that gave God the occasion to raise Jesus from the dead and constitute him Lord of honor or glory.

Who are the "rulers of this age" who crucified the Lord of glory but are passing away? There are three opinions: human rulers, demonic powers, and human rulers as the instruments of demonic powers. Perhaps the latter is the most probable meaning. A typical man of Mediterranean culture,

Paul believed in a host of personal malevolent forces who wage deadly combat against God's holy ones: Death (1 Cor 15:26), Sin (Rom 5:21), Satan (1 Cor 5:5), Rulers (1 Cor 2:6, 8), Tempters (1 Thess 3:5), Demons (1 Cor 10:20-21), Angels (1 Cor 6:3), Spirits (1 Cor 2:12), and gods (2 Cor 4:4). Curiously, Paul never speaks of "the Devil" or of an "unclean spirit," terms found in the Gospels. Nevertheless, Paul is convinced these forces are responsible for leading the so-called "mature" people astray as well as instigating the rulers who crucified the Lord of honor. Had they known God's plan, they would not have put Jesus to death.

In the gospel (Matt 5:17-33), Jesus broadens the reach of the Commandments in order to flesh out the requirements of God's plan of salvation. It is a wisdom even the most sophisticated—like those in Corinth—could not have discovered with their own abilities. It is a wisdom intended for all. Do contemporary believers distinguish between elites and privileged in contrast to the less enlightened? What strategies (like Paul's irony and sarcasm) might contemporary believers employ to obliterate such distinctions?

Seventh Sunday in Ordinary Time
1 Corinthians 3:16-23

Here is a text-segment that Americans almost always misinterpret. The reasons are linguistic and cultural. From a linguistic perspective, the Greek "you's" in v. 16 are plural. The English language doesn't distinguish well between singular and plural "you," hence the translation causes confusion and misunderstanding because it doesn't indicate the plural. Paul refers to the community (plural) not the individual (singular). The community is God's residence (Temple) in which the power of God (God's Spirit) is housed. That house or temple is holy; therefore, holy are you (plural), you the social body, the community. If anyone destroys God's community, God will destroy that person. The punishment is the law of talion, a tit-for-tat. That is how precious God considers the community.

The cultural reason for American misinterpretation is the high value Americans place on individualism. This perspective is very rare on this planet represented by barely 20 percent of its total population. The vast majority of people on this planet live in collectivistic cultures; that is, cultures in which the individual is subservient to the community. In such cultures, individuals are dyadic or collectivistic personalities. Their individual identity derives from the community. Because the community is holy, its members participate in that holiness just as family members share in family honor.

Mediterranean cultures in general are collectivistic. In such a social context, the Spirit can never be private property, a personal possession. The Spirit belongs to the group, informs the group, makes the group its temple, and makes the group holy.

How is this holy community profaned or destroyed? By deceit or masquerade. In Galatians (6:3) Paul enunciates a general rule: "If any one think he is something when he is nothing, he is deluding himself." To the Corinthians he declares: "If any one among you considers himself wise in this age, let him become a fool, so as to become wise" (1 Cor 3:18; see also 8:2; 14:37-38). It is not the individual, personal opinion that counts (so-called "self"-esteem), but rather the community that bestows identity upon a collectivistic or dyadic personality according to what the community perceives.

Finally, Paul the trained Pharisee quotes impressively from the tradition: Job 5:13 and Psalm 94:11 to demonstrate his conviction that God is reversing the map of honor. God's ideas of honor differ from the culture's ideas. In God's view, foolishness (the message of the cross, 1:18) is the power of God and therefore honor. The conclusion is obvious: no one should boast! Stoics believed: "All things belong to the wise" (Diogenes Laertius: *Vit.* 7:125). Paul suggests an alternative: "Everything belongs to you, you to Christ, and Christ to God."

The gospel (Matt 5:35-48) is a continuation of Jesus' Sermon on the Mount in which Jesus challenges the law of talion within the community (Matt 5:38-42). How would Jesus' challenge affect Paul's position that God operates by law of talion toward those insiders who harm the community? How should modern believers behave toward insiders who harm the community or its members? Ought a believer behave differently toward outsiders? Is the Mediterranean cultural distinction between insider and outsider acceptable in Western culture?

Eighth Sunday in Ordinary Time
1 Corinthians 4:1-5

Pauline scholar Murphy-O'Connor notes that in these verses (as in other places in 1 Corinthians 1–4), Paul adopts a tactic of ridicule and cruel laughter against the "spirit people" (see Sixth Sunday in Ordinary Time, Year A). While this might offend Western sensibilities (Murphy-O'Connor calls it "lack of charity," thus failing to understand the nature of Mediterranean culture), it is important to remember that Paul and his opponents lived in an agonistic culture. People learn how to give (insult, for example) as good as they get. The more effectively one can ridicule (shame) an opponent, the greater will be one's honor-rating. In comparison with Apollos, Paul pales as a speaker. Apollos was the champion of the spirit-people not only because of his rhetorical skill but apparently because of the "superior" wisdom he imparted compared to Paul's preaching. Paul's reputation was at stake. The majority of Corinthians who were not spirit people were keenly interested to see how Paul would defend his honor.

In an honor culture, the best defense is an offense. Paul's retort to the spirit people is tantamount to "Who died and put you in charge?": "It does not concern me in the least that I be judged by you" (1 Cor 4:3). The Corinthians did not hire or appoint him, and Paul did not assume his position on his own ("I do not even pass judgment on myself"). His role is to be "servant of Christ" and "steward of the mysteries of God." The idea behind servant (besides service) is "official witness" (to the Messiah). A steward is basically one who oversees possessions, business affairs, servants, etc. Paul is expected to oversee the mysteries of God, another way to describe the core of the Christian gospel revealed now to apostles. He is, therefore, accountable to God alone. The people who think they possess superior wisdom do not have the foggiest idea about the basis for Paul's ministry and his honor claims.

How will this be resolved? When the Lord comes everything will be made clear. Remember that this culture thrives on secrecy, deception, and lies. Who can know the truth? The Lord "will bring to light what is hidden in darkness" (v. 5; compare Matt 10:26). Recall also that this non-introspective culture judges only by externals. The Corinthians judge Paul only by his appearance, his speech-patterns, and the like. God and only God knows the human heart (1 Sam 16:7), and the Lord "will manifest the motives of our hearts" (v. 5). The end result is that everyone who deserves it will receive praise (= true honor) from God.

In today's gospel (Matt 6:24-34), Jesus repeatedly exhorts his listeners not to be anxious (or worry) about life (food, clothes, the morrow), for God will surely take care. Jesus left it all in God's hands. Paul trusted in God, too, but he also used his skills of ridicule and insult to secure his honor. Which option would you choose?

Ninth Sunday
in Ordinary Time
Romans 3:21-25, 28

[For introductory comments see Fourth Sunday of Advent.]
From Rom 1:18 to 3:20, Paul presents "bad news"; that is, a
very gloomy picture of hopelessness for human existence apart
from Messiah Jesus. At this point (3:21), Paul introduces the
Good News: God presents a much simpler way of setting
people in right relationship to the deity, namely through
unswerving loyalty (faith in) Messiah Jesus (v. 22) in whom
the divine quality of uprightness is revealed. All who have
faith appropriate this uprightness to themselves according to
the divine plan.

What is striking in Paul's statement is his emphasis on "all."
All who have sinned are deprived of God's glory, and all
who believe are justified freely by faith. It stands in contrast
to the opinion of Rabbi Simeon bar-Yoai (third-generation
Tanna, ca. A.D. 130–160) who describes God thus: "I am
God over all that comes into the world, but I have joined my
name only with you. I am not called the God of the Gentiles,
but the God of Israel" (Exodus Rabbah 29). Paul insists that
the one God is God of all: Israelites and non-Israelites as well.

Two other questions quite likely occur to all who read
these verses. One: sometimes it seems that Paul writes very
obtuse sentences. Verses 24-25 in the lectionary are certainly
an example: "They [all who have sinned] are justified freely
by his grace through the redemption in Christ Jesus, whom

41

God set forth as an expiation, through faith, by his blood"
(Revised NAB). What in the world does this mean in plain
English? Why does Paul write like this?

Paul writes just as a typical Eastern Mediterranean man of
his time and culture thinks and speaks. These people are not
only non-introspective but anti-introspective. They do not
have any hidden thoughts. They speak first and think slightly
later. In other words, Paul is thinking on his feet and speaking in a stream-of-consciousness fashion. There is no internal control or censorship over what will come directly from
his mind out of his mouth. The Greek does not make much
better sense than the English translations.

Well, can we gain some idea of what Paul is trying to communicate in these verses? The broader context make his
central point clear. We already mentioned it above: God
brings sinners back to right relationship with the deity through
unswerving loyalty (faith) in Messiah Jesus. How? The key
word here is "blood," the blood of Jesus. In Israelite tradition, "the life of a living body is in its blood" and "it is the
blood, as the seat of life, that makes atonement" (Lev 17:11).
This central element of life belongs to the deity alone. When
offered in sacrifice to God it can produce one of two effects:
life-maintenance or life-restoration.

Just as feuding between human beings requires some recon-
ciliation to keep life-threat (vengeance) at bay and reestablish
life-supporting relations, so Jesus' blood works this effect (called
"expiation" in v. 25) with God. Jesus' blood now has a life-effect
in terms of life-restoration. Redemption (v. 25) is the restora-
tion of the honor of God's people (considered by Paul to be
"all" who sinned but who now have faith in Jesus Messiah).

In today's gospel (Matt 7:21-27), as he concludes the Sermon on the Mount, Matthew's Jesus encourages his listeners
who culturally prefer spontaneous activity ("Lord, Lord!"
saying the right thing to the right person at the right time, like
an automatic salute by a soldier to an officer) to consider re-
placing that with planned and calculated activity: doing the
will of the Father (7:21). Paul offers a clarification for his listeners: doing the will of the Father, or staying right with God,
comes through "faith apart from works of the law."

Tenth Sunday in Ordinary Time
Romans 4:18-25

In Romans 4, Paul uses Abraham to illustrate his point that uprightness with God derives from faith. Abraham was considered upright because of his faith (vv. 1-8) rather than because of his circumcision (vv. 9-12). Righteousness came to Abraham in virtue of a promise (vv. 13-17), hence he is a model of faith for those who have accepted Jesus as Messiah.

In the first century, a popular Israelite belief claimed that Abraham knew and obeyed the Torah even though he lived long before God revealed it to Moses. Paul challenges this belief. About twenty-nine years after God declared Abraham to be upright (see Genesis 15), Abraham was circumcised (see Genesis 17). Throughout this passage Paul repeats that Abraham trusted in God (= hope) and remained firmly loyal to God (= faith), which God "credited to him as righteousness."

Paul does something in today's verses that every modern believer wants to do and often does: makes an immediate application "to us." He does this by means of midrashic interpretation. The word *midrash* in post-biblical Hebrew means to explain or interpret Scripture based, of course, on study (see Sir 51:23: "the house of instruction" reflects the Hebrew phrase *beth hammidrash*). One purpose of midrash is to modernize or actualize (to use a modern term) the Old Testament by applying it to a new situation. To do this, Paul emphasizes that Abraham had faith while he completely ignores elements of Abraham's skepticism, e.g., like falling on his face and

laughing to hear that at ninety-nine years of age he would produce a son with his ninety-year-old wife (Gen 17:17).

Paul is more interested in playing with the word "dead."
Abraham's body and Sarah's womb were "dead," but God
brought life from these dead elements. Thus Abraham's faith
in God foreshadowed the kind of faith Paul's contempo-
raries have that God raised Jesus from the dead. Similarly,
the consequences for the believer then are new life gained
through the death and resurrection of Jesus.

In today's gospel (Matt 9:9-13), Jesus quotes a proverb, joins
a quote from Hos 6:6 to it, and tells his critics to "go and learn
the meaning of these words [from Hosea]" (v. 13). Modern believers face the very same challenge. Separated by time and
culture from the scenarios in the Bible, contemporary preachers are obliged to bridge those and other gaps in order to determine a culturally plausible interpretation of text-segments.
They cannot be selective or uncritical as Paul was in interpretation.* Only then can the preacher or teacher begin to explore
cross-cultural applications to modern situations.

(*This evaluation of Paul is admittedly somewhat anachro-
nistic. Even in modern times, midrash remains a key element
of Jewish interpretation of the Bible. It is part of the method
by which Jewish interpreters make ancient texts relevant to
modern life. In contrast, most Christian and all Catholic interpretation is committed to historical-critical methods of interpretation which sharply distinguishes it from Jewish
methods. It is also possible to make ancient texts relevant to
modern life with historical critical methods, but the process
is somewhat more complex. For the view of the Catholic
Church, see the Pontifical Biblical Commission document
"The Interpretation of the Bible in the Church," 1994, on the
Internet at: http://clawww.lmu.edu/faculty/fjust/Docs/PBC
_Interp.htm. Also see Pilch 1994.)

First Sunday of Lent
Romans 5:12-19

[Preachers and other readers must be careful not to impose on vv. 12-14 the refined contemporary understanding of the dogma of Original Sin. While Trent (see Session V, 2–4, echoing the Sixteenth Council of Carthage [A.D. 418] and the Second Council of Carthage [A.D. 529]) said these verses do teach a form of the dogma, one must be fair to Paul who did not even use the phrase "original sin." That originated with Augustine. The reality of the sin and its universal terrible impact on all creation are a constant throughout history. Regarding other aspects of this notion, there were significant differences in the tradition.]

In this text-segment, we recognize a familiar thought pattern that recurs in the Pauline literature: then and now; the period of Adam, Sin, and Death (then), and the period of Jesus, righteousness, and life (now). Sin reigned from Adam until Jesus Messiah; Jesus' obedience ended that reign and inaugurated a new period of grace.

Sin and Death in these paragraphs are personifications. Sin is an active force within and among all human beings. As Paul notes, it has been present since the very beginnings of the human race. In the Israelite understanding, Sin expresses itself chiefly through the "flesh." Flesh is not a synonym for body but rather describes a person from the perspective of unredeemed weakness. Death is also a personified, cosmic force which has two effects: it destroys the human body and causes definitive separation from God. Thus for Paul, Sin is the twin of Death.

Paul's main interest is not Sin and Death but rather Adam and Jesus. He contrasts the two. The world was changed by each. Adam unleashed into the world an active hostile force (Sin) which had the power to cause definitive alienation from God (Death), the source of all life. The force (Sin) was accepted and ratified by all individuals who sinned through personal, actual misdeeds (v. 12). In contrast, Jesus's redemptive death unleashed uprightness and life for all who accept (believe in) him. The tragedy of Adam's failure is offset by the magnificent plenitude of Jesus' redemption.

The far-reading perverse consequences of Adam's disobedience are reported according to a rabbinic model that divided time into three periods. The first extended from Adam to Moses, during which time there was no law to disobey (v. 14). Still, Adam's transgression was so powerful that the death it caused (separation from God) dominated. All humanity during the period lived in Sin and subjection to Death. The second extended from Moses to the Messiah, during which the law occasioned many transgressions. The third period from the Messiah onward brought the gracious gift of one, Jesus the Messiah, that resulted in acquittal, justification, but above all, life for all. Humanity in the image of the new Adam enjoys God's righteousness and "reigns in life."

The traditional gospel account read on this Sunday of Lent is the Testing of Jesus (Matt 4:1-11). These are not temptations to sin but rather tests of loyalty. Will he really prove to be the beloved Son as identified in the baptism with whom the Father is "well pleased" (see Matt 3:17)? Already prior to his death and resurrection, Jesus is reversing the disobedience of Adam. If the good life has been made so readily available to all, why do so few avail themselves of it?

Second Sunday of Lent
2 Timothy 1:8b-10

In 2 Tim 1:6–2:23, the Pastor who wrote around 100 A.D. in the name of Paul presents Paul as a model of steadfastness in persecution. This is necessary because Timothy has become very discouraged–indeed ashamed!–and has begun to fall short of being an ideal Church leader. Verse 8a exhorts Timothy: "Do not be ashamed of your testifying to the Lord, nor of me [Paul]!" It's definitely a wake-up call. Today's verses which follow immediately present Paul as a model. God saved Paul not because of anything Paul did but rather freely through grace bestowed in Jesus according to God's plan at the very beginning. Jesus destroyed the power of death and brought life and immortality to humanity. The charge to Timothy: "Bear the hardships you encounter in sharing the gospel because God gives the strength to endure!"

The transfiguration of Jesus reported in today's gospel (Matt 17:1-9) was intended to inform the doubting disciples about Jesus' true identity and to strengthen their commitment to continue with Jesus in his mission. Lacking an altered-state-of-consciousness experience like this, Timothy needed the concrete example of Paul and the strong exhortation of the Pastor: bear your suffering! Who among us can exhort others when their commitment flags to take courage and continue the commitment?

Third Sunday of Lent
Romans 5:1-2, 5-8

[For introductory comments see Fourth Sunday of Advent.] A new emphasis emerges in chapter five of Romans. Previously Paul spoke of the utter hopelessness of human existence without Jesus Messiah (1:18–3:20), then salvation through faith in Jesus Messiah (3:21–4:25). Now Paul reflects on the life of a person who has accepted Jesus as Messiah. In chapter five justification and righteousness recede from major consideration, while God's love comes to the fore. In today's select verses, Paul considers how it feels to be right with God.

The two principal effects of being in right relationship with God are peace (v. 1) and hope (v. 2). The peace Paul speaks of is that calm and relief which human beings experience after wrestling with and resolving great doubts or problems. In the anti-introspective culture of the Middle East, doubts and other such problems tend to be externalized, that is, somatized. When they are resolved, the results bring peace and restore wholesomeness and physical health.

Hope or trust is confidence to such a degree that one puts everything into the hands of the trusted person. Here, the object of such hope or trust is the confidence of sharing in God's honor. Paul boasts about this hope. In the Bible, boasting is the way in which one acknowledges one's personal lord and master; in this case, God. If through sin a person has shamed God and become thereby a shameful person, what a remarkable reversal of life-situation it is to share now in the immeasurable honor and glory of God. This is truly an amazing gift from God. Indeed, Paul goes on to explain this in vv. 5-8. That Jesus, who didn't deserve to die this death, agreed to die for sinners is an incredible thought. In a cultural world which operates predominantly by informal exchanges known as dyadic contract (I do you a favor, you owe me. You repay the favor, I owe you; etc.), that Jesus would do us a favor which is truly impossible for us to repay is absolutely astonishing. Yet, that is indeed how God proves his love for us. God's ways are not the ways of human beings.

The familiar story of the Samaritan woman who met Jesus at the well (John 4:5-42) illustrates this same point. She who had no reason to anticipate the outcome of her dialogue with a traditional enemy (a Judean) was so touched that she went to the town, related her experience, and "boasted": "Come see a man who told me everything I have done. Could he be the Messiah?" (v. 29, see also v. 39). To receive and appreciate unmerited benevolence causes profound changes in human life. What else can one do but acknowledge one's lord and master? What else can one do but boast?

Fourth Sunday of Lent
Ephesians 5:8-14

In this segment of his letter, the sacred author waiting in Paul's name between 80–100 A.D. elaborates upon Eph 4:17, that these believers should "no longer live as the Gentiles do" but should "try to learn what is pleasing to the Lord" (v. 10). The image he uses is familiar to us from the Qumran Literature: light and darkness. Members of that community are directed "to love all the sons of light, each one according to his lot in God's plan, and to detest all the sons of darkness, each one in accordance with his blame in God's vindication" (1QS 1:9-11). The sacred author of Ephesians exhorts the letter recipients to "live as children of light" producing "every kind of goodness and righteousness and truth."

The children of light are encouraged to "rebuke" (lectionary: "expose") those who perform the works of darkness. Culturally speaking, simply to expose wrongdoing is certainly shameful but to make a public scene over it and "convict" that person is even more shameful. In fact, it is the limit to which a person will push in "exposing" deeds of darkness. This was also an important task at Qumran:

> He [God] knows the result of his deeds for all times everlasting and has given them as legacy to the sons of men so that they know good [and evil], so that they decide the lot of every living being in compliance with the spirit there is in him [at the time of] the visitation (1QS 4:25-26; compare Matt 18:15-17).

He concludes with a fragment of a baptismal hymn (v. 14). This reflection fits well with the theme of light and sight in today's gospel (John 9:1-41). It is well to remember that while this imagery of light and darkness was evidently quite popular and widely used, the imagery reflected a reality: proper behavior that is pleasing to God.

Fifth Sunday of Lent
Romans 8:8-11

[See also Fourteenth Sunday in Ordinary Time; for some background to Romans see Fourth Sunday of Advent]. Today we encounter another set of contrasting words that Paul likes to use in discussing the human condition: flesh and spirit. Flesh connotes natural, concretely material human existence. In these verses it is equivalent to slavery and suggests something outside of God's realm. Paul connects flesh with Death: "the concern of the flesh is death" (Rom 8:6). Moreover, "the concern of the flesh is hostility toward God; it does not submit to the law of God, nor can it; and those who are in the flesh cannot please God" (Rom 8:7-8). It is a rather depressing picture. In contrast, spirit denotes freedom and suggests things of God and heaven. It is the very power which raised Jesus' human and mortal body from death to holiness and life (Rom 8:10).

The Israelite tradition believed that human beings were pulled in two different directions or ways by different spirits: good ones and evil ones. Human beings are caught in the middle of a battle that never ends: in the heavens, on earth, and within the individual person. The question is: Which spirit will "lord" it over a person? The same is true of the ongoing struggle between flesh and spirit. "For the flesh has desires against the Spirit, and the Spirit against the flesh" (Gal 5:17). Romans 8:1-17, which describes the workings of God's Spirit unto salvation, balances the preceding section (Rom

7:7-12) in which Paul describes himself at the mercy of a force that is not of God. From this perspective, the reader can sense and appreciate Paul's relief and the urgency with which he exhorts the letter recipients to live by the Spirit.

The familiar report of Jesus raising Lazarus from the dead (John 11:1-45) is not only appropriate for this lenten season but also relates well with these thoughts from Paul. The Spirit which will eventually raise Jesus from the dead is already at work in the raising of Lazarus. Paul knows experientially the power of the Spirit and tries to communicate it to his letter recipients. Paul would echo for modern believers the words of Martha to Jesus: "What you [Jesus] ask of God, God will give you." All we need do is ask.

Palm Sunday
of the Lord's Passion
Philippians 2:6-11

[Contemporary scholarship identifies three distinct letters in Philippians: Letter A = 4:10-20 (in which Paul acknowledges receiving a gift; it is a receipt for aid); Letter B = 1:1–3:1a; 4:4-7, 21-23 (in which Paul having heard of problems in the community exhorts to unity and joy); and Letter C = 3:1b–4:3, 8-9 (in which Paul addresses problems caused by wandering Judaizing missionaries). Scholars who identify three letters, date A and B probably from 54–57 A.D.; Letter C some time later, perhaps 57–58 A.D. All came from Paul imprisoned in Ephesus. Those who identify two letters (combining B and C into one–B), date A to 58–60 A.D., and B to 62 A.D. when Paul was imprisoned in Rome.] Intra-community squabbles about how to live the gospel threatened to divide the Philippians. Paul exhorts them to put aside differences, close ranks, and pursue the virtue of humility after the pattern of Jesus (vv. 1-5). Then, in this well-known hymn (vv. 6-11), Paul presents Jesus as a model for the Philippians to imitate. Scholars agree that this hymn was composed prior to and independently of this letter. It has two sections: vv. 6-8 describe Jesus' humiliation (a shameful thing in this culture), while vv. 9-11 tell how God exalted him to unimaginable honor. Paul uses this hymn to exert moral pressure on the Philippians.

Many commentators see in v. 6 an implicit contrast between Adam who wanted to exploit likeness to God for selfish purposes and Jesus who did not. The verses contain many allusions to Genesis 1–3. In the Israelite tradition, being godlike means being immune from death (Wis 2:23). These verses compare the human Jesus with the human Adam (it is not a reference to pre-existent Jesus who became human). They contrast Jesus' refusal as the final Adam to seek equality with God but highlight his humility and obedience to God in accepting mortality with the first Adam's arrogance and disobedience. He sought to be equal to God as immortal, disobeyed God, and was cursed by God.

By his shameful death, Jesus was humiliated, a major tragedy in this honor driven culture. But God loved Jesus and exalted him. Thus the basic meaning of Jesus who died and was raised is that he was humiliated and exalted, by God of course. The phrase "on the cross" disturbs the poetry of the hymn and was very likely added by Paul to underscore the degree of Jesus' humiliation. In response (vv. 9-11), God exalted Jesus to rule over the entire universe. Jesus is Lord, the same word used in the Greek Bible to be spoken instead of Yhwh. The one who in total obedience took on the low rank of slave now by God's own commission is universal Lord.

To appreciate this hymn, one needs to remember some key elements of honor cultures. First, although one is rightly entitled to ascribed honor (usually by birth), it is also important not to give the impression that one seeks to augment that honor by impinging on others. Thus, all people learn to practice "cultural humility," that is, staying one step behind one's rightful place. Others clearly see that such a person is no threat to their honor. More than this, others will summon this person to his or her rightful, honorable place.

Though this hymn may appear on a surface reading to reflect the reward of cultural humility, in actuality it does not. The hymn rather points to value reversal: shame leads to honor. In other words, Jesus didn't just politely state his humility, confident that someone would raise him to his proper place. He willingly accepted humiliation in the manner of his death. This is something Jesus' culture would not only not have expected but also would not have encouraged. Thus, any culture like that of our ancestors in the faith who live by honor and shame values would be "shocked" by this message of value-reversal: shame will lead to honor. This hymn presents that notion masterfully. It is likely that with this hymn Paul intended to propose an example for the Philippians to imitate given the situation in which they found themselves.

A second consideration is to keep in mind that Philippi was a Roman colony most of whose citizens were retired from the military. They had strong ties to Rome and would be quite willing to participate in the imperial cult, that is, acknowledging Caesar as divine. It is therefore plausible that Paul is vigorously arguing against such participation. His use of certain words (Lord), proposed gestures (bending the knee), mention of an empire (Phil 2:10), and the acclamation "Jesus is Lord" all echo the language of the imperial cult but speak instead of Jesus. Paul is deliberately commanding the Philippians to acknowledge Jesus as Lord rather than Caesar. This, however, is a treasonous act. What course of action would a retired military person who is devoted to Rome but believes in Jesus choose?

Finally, the downward-upward movement of Jesus' life (humiliation/exaltation; Phil 2:6-8, 9-11) is reflected in Paul's life. He voluntarily abandons all advantages (Phil 3:4-8) in obedience to God. Then, as slave of God (Phil 1:1), Paul carries this obedience (Phil 1:16) to the point that he might—like Jesus—die a shameful death (Phil 1:20) confident that his glory is to come (Phil 3:10-11). The pattern resonates in the lives of Timothy and Epaphroditus as well. The three live in unselfish obedience and service and are a foil to the self-seeking and selfishness that have crept into the Philippian church.

Of course, today's gospel (Matt 26:14–27:66), the Passion of Jesus, presents in significantly more detail the shameful end of Jesus' life which God reversed a short while later. It also reflects the choice Jesus made between acknowledging his identity and relationship to God and capitulating to his interrogators. Value reversal is a sobering meditation for people in any culture. So too is loyalty. Holy Week provides yet another opportunity to reflect on the death of Jesus and the challenge it poses to all believers.

Easter Sunday–Easter Vigil
Romans 6:3-11

[See John J. Pilch, *The Triduum and Easter Sunday: Breaking Open the Scriptures* (Collegeville: The Liturgical Press, 2000).]

In Romans 5–8 Paul highlights God's love and exhorts the believers living in Rome to "consider yourselves dead to sin and alive to God in Christ Jesus" (6:11). Sin in the singular is noteworthy. Paul is not talking about some sort of human failing. Rather, his Greek word for sin is more correctly understood as a force or a power that drives a person toward an almost unavoidable proneness to failure or to committing an evil deed. Remember that Mediterranean culture views human beings as subject to nature rather than as controlling nature. Nature, in the Mediterranean world, includes an invisible world of powers and forces which mischievously, capriciously, or sometimes even with deliberate calculation intervene in human life and cause human beings to behave in ways that displease God. This world of power and forces is the context in which Paul understands sin.

The good news in Paul's passage is that Jesus' death and resurrection have destroyed the effectiveness of this force or power called sin. Furthermore, baptism snatches believers from the power of this force and incorporates them into new life with God. This is something very real and very welcome in the Mediterranean way of thinking. While some people in this world use amulets, gestures, or incantations to ward off evil, believers through baptism are intimately united with the very one who has defeated the source of all evil.

But people still fail and still commit sins. It is to this situation that Paul speaks when he exhorts his letter-recipients thus: thanks to baptism our old self was crucified (v. 6) and we are now "alive to God in Christ Jesus" (v. 11); therefore, we should live accordingly.

Easter Sunday
Colossians 3:1-4 or 1 Corinthians 5:6b-8

[Modern scholars locate this letter among the Deutero-Paulines written between 70 and 80 A.D. by someone who knew the Pauline tradition quite well. Perhaps it is a product of a Pauline school tradition located in Ephesus. Colossians 1:14 speaks of "forgiveness of sins," one of thirty-eight such words or phrase which occur nowhere in the undisputed Pauline writings (see Eph 1:7; Heb 9:22; 10:18), supporting the argument against authenticity as a letter of Paul.]

Colossians 3:1-4. Written by a creative admirer of Paul perhaps between A.D. 63 and 90, this letter presents Jesus as the cosmic Messiah and explains what it means for believers to be exclusively devoted to his service. The letter is addressed to believers living in Colossae, a town in southwestern Turkey near Laodicea not far from modern Pammukale. Today's verses begin the paraenetic, that is, hortatory section of the letters. The message is simple. Since believers through baptism have been raised with Jesus, they ought to focus on matters pertaining to alternate reality (what is above) rather than getting bogged down in material reality (the world in which we live). Today's gospel has some consequences for the ordinary life of the believer: this selection from Colossians puts those consequences in focus.

[For background, see Second Sunday in Ordinary Time.]

1 Corinthians 5:6b-8. This most appropriate reading for the feast of the Resurrection is drawn from the letter in which Paul deals more extensively with the physical, human body than in any other letter. For the most part, Paul is concerned with orifices. Our ancestors in the faith realized that orifices were weak points on the body through which it could be penetrated and therefore polluted. In 1 Corinthians 5–7 he focuses on the genitals, a major bodily orifice. The fuller context of today's reading (vv. 1-8) is an incestuous marriage or concubinage between a man and his stepmother. Today's verses have been carved away from this larger segment.

Paul draws an analogy between the effect of yeast and the social consequences of this incestuous union ("not found even among pagans!"). The ancients did not fully understand the fermentation process stimulated by yeast in dough and in saccharine liquids, but they knew how to make practical use of yeast in leavening bread and brewing beer. In Paul's view, the incestuous relationship is a pollutant that threatens the social body, that is, the community of believers, and the marriage partner.

In today's verses, Paul presents the rationale for his thinking. Christ the Paschal Lamb has ended the time of leaven, "the old yeast, the yeast of malice and wickedness." Therefore, it is time to get rid of that old yeast as Israelites did at Passover time. Christians are called to be a new lump of dough, yeast-free, "unleavened bread of sincerity and truth." They must strive to maintain the unity of the social body of the Church. This, of course, is the point of the feast we celebrate today, the resurrection of Jesus, which has important behavioral consequences for the community and all its individual members.

Second Sunday of Easter
1 Peter 1:3-9

This letter was sent probably between the years A.D. 75 and 92 by a group in Rome (Peter [scholars doubt that Peter was a co-author of this letter], 1:1; Silvanus, 5:12; and Mark, 5:13) to fellow believers in Jesus Messiah living in Asia Minor who are identified as "visiting strangers" (1:1; 2:11; the lectionary renders the Greek word as "sojourners") and "resident aliens" (2:11; see 1:17). These phrases describe the real-life political situation of this letter's original recipients. The peculiar accents, puzzling customs, and suspicious behaviors of strangers were quite naturally perceived to be threats to established peace, order, and well being in the community through which strangers passed. Strangers were perceived to be dangerous and therefore normal targets of unofficial expressions of discrimination and disadvantage.

In contrast, resident aliens were strangers who settled in the land. They were no longer just passing through. Even so, natives considered them to be inferior. Therefore they were granted very limited legal and social rights. Biblical characters who were resident aliens include Abraham among the Hittites (Gen 23:4), Moses in the land of Midian (Exod 2:22), and the Israelites in Egypt (Gen 15:13). Aliens were restricted in whom they could marry, the types of business they could conduct, the holding of land and successful transfer of property to kin, the right to vote, and the formation of associations and guilds. They also had to pay higher taxes and tribute.

In effect, these people had no political guarantees. They were excluded from popular assemblies and subject to more severe forms of civil punishment.

Though some strangers and resident aliens lived in the cities, the majority resided in the rural regions of the interior. The social discrimination they experienced encouraged them to form clubs and labor guilds for mutual protection, support, and acceptance. Often these associations involved shared religious belief and worship as well. This was particularly true of those believers who were converts from Judaism and paganism.

These visiting strangers and resident aliens accepted Jesus as Messiah and joined a group of believers that provided a form of human community, social unity, and acceptance that was not available to them in society. They also realized they had received the favor and acceptance of the God of Israel. They were reborn (1:3, 23; 2:2) children (1:14; 2:10) of a heavenly Father (1:2, 3, 17; 4:17) united into one household of God (2:5; 4:17) or family-like community (2:17; 2:18–5:5; 5:12-13).

These verses constitute a blessing or benediction, perhaps reflecting synagogue worship which also begins and ends with a benediction. New birth through baptism produces a living hope made possible by God's raising Jesus from the dead (v. 3), an inheritance secure in heaven and linked to a plot of soil like the holy yet profaned Land of Israel (v. 4), and a salvation now about to be revealed in this final age to those who are guarded by God's power (v. 5).

Suffering is a cause for rejoicing because these are various trials by which God is "testing" and purifying the genuineness of loyalty to the deity (= faith). Loyalty that passes the test will redound to the believers' praise, glory, and honor at the revelation of Jesus Messiah. Today's gospel (John 20:19-31) recounts an appearance of Jesus raised from the dead. The epistolary reading offers further reflection for believers upon the effects of the resurrection of Jesus and what meaning that gives to suffering in life.

Third Sunday of Easter
1 Peter 1:17-21

Reborn children of God described in last Sunday's reading have obligations that result from this new identity. They must be obedient to their new divine Father who, like a human father, is the model of their holiness. They are to conduct themselves with "reverence" (literally fear, but perhaps better "reverent awe"; see 2:17, 19; 3:2, 14, 15) toward their Father and Judge because this redemption obtained with the precious blood of Christ is the ground of their faith and hope in God.

The emphasis in 1 Peter on the concept of holiness (1:1, 14-20; 2:4-10; 3:5, 15) is a carefully selected strategy for defining the unique character and conduct of God's covenant community. Israelite groups among which those who believed in Jesus as Messiah lived, notably the community at Qumran, the Pharisees, and after A.D. 70 rabbinic Judaism as a whole, all claimed to be the one and only holy people of God. They looked down upon other groups. Thus the holy behavior stressed in these verses is aimed at separating believers in Jesus Messiah from Israelites and from pagans. Only loyalty to (= faith in) Jesus Messiah gives one admission to the holy family of God. It is faith, regardless of Israelite privilege or pagan conviction, that makes this community open to all people.

In today's gospel (Luke 24:13-35), the disciples on the road to Emmaus needed to have the Scriptures opened to them so that they might understand who Jesus is and what his death and resurrection accomplished for believers. First Peter renders the same service for the strangers and resident aliens in Asia Minor. What does it accomplish for the modern believer?

Fourth Sunday of Easter
1 Peter 2:20b-25

It is important to restore the fuller context of these verses, namely the preceding verses 18-20a. The sacred author addresses household slaves in the homes of believers. The word used to refer to these slaves placed special emphasis on their location in a household. Ordinarily in other New Testament exhortations (e.g., Col 3:18–4:1; 5:22–6:9; 1 Tim 2:8–6:2; Titus 2:1-10), slaves (and their masters) are addressed last, thus reflecting social rank. Here they are mentioned first. Therefore, through their association with the suffering Lord (vv. 21-25), they become an example for the entire household of faith.

By suffering patiently though they are doing good, such believers represent the predicament of the entire suffering community. Life for these strangers and resident aliens in Asia Minor was no picnic. Perseverance in doing good even in the face of undeserved suffering is to follow the example left for believers by Jesus. The details of Jesus' suffering are distilled from the Passion tradition and shaped after the model of the Servant Song of Isaiah 52:13–53:12. The basic idea is non-retaliation for injuries unjustly received. The sacred author concludes with the image of straying sheep gathered together by the Shepherd-Guardian (see 5:4, and the shepherd images in John 10:10-18; Heb 13:20; and Rev 7:17), which offers a "loose-link" to the gospel.

Fifth Sunday of Easter
1 Peter 2:4-9

This is a marvelous yet complex passage emphasizing the ancient covenant theme of divine election (vv. 4, 5, 6, 9). It begins (vv. 4-5) by announcing, combining, and applying both to Jesus and the believers the sacred titles that follow (vv. 4-5a refer to vv. 6-8, and the rest of 5 refers to vv. 9-10). Verses 6-8 draw on one set of traditions (Isa 28:16; Ps 118:22; Isa 8:14) that concern a "stone" which both in Israelite and Messianist traditions was considered an image of the Messiah (Mark 12:1-12 and parallels; Acts 4:8-12; Rom 9:30-33). Verses 9-10 draw on another set of traditions (Exod 19:6; Isa 43:20-21; 42:6-9; 63:7-9; Hos 1:6, 9; 2:1-12) that describe God's elect community and family but are now applied to the new people of God.

Faith in the Messiah, a living stone, makes believers living stones which God builds into a household of the Spirit, a holy priestly community. The elected people of the covenant who once formed the dwelling place of God now constitute the family in whom God's Spirit resides. As a consequence, these people of God can offer acceptable sacrifices motivated by the Spirit.

In his historical setting, Martin Luther interpreted this text as the biblical basis for a concept of the general priesthood of all believers. His point was that baptism makes priests and kings of all the faithful and that ministry is every believer's divine calling. His interpretation was a response to the situation of the church of his day and his aim of ecclesial reform. In its own first-century literary and historical setting, these verses carry a different meaning. Election of Jesus and the community is stressed much more than priesthood. In fact, the priesthood theme is mentioned nowhere in the rest of the letter, while covenant remains the dominant theme. Further, these verses carry an unmistakable collectivist stamp (dwelling place, household, priestly community, nation, people) true to the collectivistic understanding of personality that prevailed in Asia Minor. The passage does not affirm the equality of all believers as individual priests or kings. Hence the emphasis is on the community and the divine favor accorded to the new covenant people of God.

In today's gospel (John 14:1-12), Jesus focuses the disciples' attention on the Father and the Father's dwelling. Jesus concludes by promising that the one who believes in him will do the works he does and even greater works. The sacred authors of 1 Peter add further insight to how believers can do the works of Jesus and even greater. What does it mean in the twenty-first century to "offer spiritual sacrifices acceptable to God through Jesus Christ"?

Sixth Sunday of Easter
1 Peter 3:15-18

In this section the sacred authors continue to emphasize the theme of doing what is right even in the face of suffering. As a community of strangers and resident aliens meeting with suspicion and slander (suffering) at every turn, the believers are urged to give an explanation (literally in Greek, "make a defense") for the extraordinary hope they have (1:3, 13, 21; 3:5). Hope in cultural context means trust, putting all one's confidence in God, not hedging one's bets. In a culture where one was expected to jockey always for establishing the best possible contacts and seeking the most influential patrons, it was mystifying to see these people remain so faithful. Believers knew that they would be vindicated by God for their loyalty, whereas the non-believers who abused the faithful would be put to shame. Again, in this culture where honor and shame are the core cultural values, the arguments of the sacred authors make eminent sense.

The pay-off for believers in real life is summed up in the final verse. Having died as all mortals must, Jesus was made alive in the Spirit who gives life (see John 5:21; 6:63; Rom 4:17; 8:11; 1 Cor 15:22). The theme and vocabulary are very familiar: flesh versus spirit, human versus divine, death-dealing versus life-giving existence (see Rom 1:3-4; 8:1-17; 1 Tim 3:16). In today's gospel (John 14:15-21) Jesus offers his disciples another insight into the Spirit, one which complements the insight in 1 Peter. In a previous generation, believers studied "apologetics" or methods and arguments for defending the faith. Today's reading proposes a different approach: believers ought to be able to explain or defend the reason for their hope, their trust, which of course is rooted in the Spirit. How might you do this?

The Ascension of the Lord
Ephesians 1:17-23

[For brief introduction, see Second Sunday after Christmas.] These verses are an intercessory prayer on behalf of the letter recipients. The chief hope of the letter writer is that believers grow in knowledge of God, God's activity, and God's gifts. God raised Jesus from the dead and gave him a place of honor next to God in the sky. This makes Jesus a co-regent or ruler with God. In Jesus' risen position he is exalted over angelic and cosmic forces which have such serious impact on the lives of ordinary human beings. Principalities, authorities, powers, and dominions are celestial personages, astral beings who are now subject to Christ. Further, Jesus is head over the church which is his body. In this letter, however, Paul's basic idea is further developed by the one who wrote in his name. Now, the church, Christ's body, benefits from God's all-embracing plan, and one of the benefits is to share in the dominion which the head, Jesus, has. Today's gospel (Matt 28:16-20) tells how at his return to the Father Jesus shared some of the power given to him with his disciples, assuring them of his presence always until the end of the age.

Seventh Sunday of Easter
1 Peter 4:13-16

As the letter moves toward a conclusion, the sacred authors remind the recipients of their bondedness by calling them "beloved" (see also 2:11). In Mediterranean culture, love does not include the idea of affection or sentiment. Rather, it describes group-embeddedness, group-glue, the bond that ties collectivistic people together. The use of "beloved" is deliberate here because the specific reason for suffering includes severe reprisal: "insulted for the name of Christ" and "suffer as a Christian."

The term "Christian" occurs only three times in the New Testament, and it is not a self-designation. Members of the believing community saw themselves as the "Israel of God" (Gal 6:16) or God's elect and holy people (1 Peter 2:9). The Latin form of the term *(Christianus)* and its first use in Syrian Antioch (Acts 11:26; see also 26:28) indicate it was first coined and applied to followers of Jesus by Latin-speaking pagans. It was clearly a derogatory term, equivalent to an English "four letter word," intended to ridicule these people infatuated with Jesus. Professor John Elliott suggests "Christ-lackeys" as a suitable rendition of the insult.

Fully appreciating how devastating such name-calling could be for these perpetually harassed believers, the sacred authors exhort them to remain steadfast. Eventually they will rejoice, even as they are now blessed. Better to suffer for this than for murder, theft, or being a wrongdoer or mischief

maker. Murder and theft are forbidden by the decalogue. Believers in Jesus should at least be as good as the group from
which they want to be distinguished, which group in turn
may have been one source of their suffering. Wrongdoer
(evildoer) contrasts with an obeyer of God's will (see 2:12,
14-15; 3:11). Mischief maker in the household of God (v. 17)
would be one who meddles in the affairs of "outsiders." Recall that people of this culture observed rigid demarcations
of boundaries, carefully separating insiders from outsiders.
The sacred author's advice here is similar to Paul's on another occasion (1 Cor 5:12-13).

In today's gospel (John 17:1-11a), Jesus prays that the
Father honor him so that he may in turn honor the Father.
The epistle similarly speaks of honor (= glory) both for the
one who suffers steadfastly and for God who is honored by
steadfast believers. Given the ineffective motivating force of
honor in Western culture, how can modern believers be per-
suaded to remain faithfully obedient to God when life takes
difficult turns?

The Vigil of Pentecost
Romans 8:22-27

According to Paul, three things persuade us of the greatness of the glory or intimate share in God's life which is the destiny of each believer: the testimony of creation (vv. 19-22), the conviction of believers (vv. 23-25), and the testimony of the Spirit (vv. 26-30). Because of Adam's sin (Gen 3:15-17), material nature was cursed, subject to decay itself just like the human beings for whom it had been created. This solidarity in punishment also entails solidarity in redemption. So creation eagerly awaits and groans in labor pains until that final state of glory will be definitively restored. This reflection has special cultural significance. In general, Mediterranean cultures of antiquity recognized that they had absolutely no control over material creation. They were subject to it; they had to suffer and endure it. Thus our ancestors in the faith believed that because of Adam's sin, human beings had no control over nature, yet the redemption of Adam would include the redemption of material creation as well.

What is the basis for Paul's confidence? He draws insight from the notion of first fruits of a harvest (vv. 23-25). When offered to God, these first fruits consecrated the entire harvest and became, as it were, down-payment, pledge, or guarantee of what was still to come. The Spirit serves this purpose for believers (vv. 26-30). Since the believer is already son/child of God (Rom 8:15), the full implementation of this status will include the redemption of the body.

In saying that "we do not know how to pray as we ought" (v. 26), Paul seems to contradict what he said just a few verses earlier, that the Spirit prompts us to pray with confidence: "Abba, my Father" (Rom 8:15). It is possible that Paul offers a corrective here to enthusiasm, namely, an exaggerated emphasis on the gifts of the Spirit. It is always possible to be overconfident. The truth is, of course, that because of natural human shortcomings, the Spirit adds its intercessions to our inadequate expressions. God knows this. In today's Gospel (John 7:37-39), John illuminates Jesus' statement as a reference to the Spirit which believers would receive. Paul in his turn explains what that Spirit does for believers.

Pentecost
1 Corinthians 12:3b-7, 12-13

[For background, see Second Sunday in Ordinary Time.] Even a cursory reading of these verses indicates that Paul is insisting on unity. The Corinthian community was so torn by competing party loyalties and dissension that Paul repeatedly exhorts to unity at every opportunity in this letter. The "spirit-people" in Corinth were viewed as the cause of disunity, in part because they were vaunting the Spirit, themselves, and their gifts from the Spirit above others who did not possess such gifts.

It is very difficult for Western individualists to appreciate the harm done by competition in a culture whose core value is honor. By birth, all people in such a culture have ascribed honor. It is shameful and wrong to attempt to improve that status. The cultural obligation is to maintain and preserve it. Cooperation, harmony, and unity are the preferred and honorable values in a collectivistic society.

The combination of verses selected as today's reading highlights two powerful arguments that Paul mounts against such divisive competition. One argument is based on how three heavenly figures relate to each other. After admitting that the Spirit does indeed grant various gifts, forms of service, and workings, Paul notes—in an apparent hierarchic ordering—that the Spirit, the Lord, and God live in harmony and not in rivalry or competition. God, of course, is sovereign and holds the highest place on the honor map (see 1 Cor 11:3;

15:27-28). And the authentic spirit acknowledges that Jesus has a special position: "Jesus is Lord." Thus, after God, Jesus enjoys the next maximum status, and the Spirit holds third place as servant of the Lord Jesus. The three are not equal in role or status, yet they live harmoniously in heaven. The Spirit and the Spirit's gifts, therefore, should not disrupt the order God has willed for the world. The second argument is based on the human body which consists of different parts, all of which must work together harmoniously lest damage occur to the body.

This exaggerated sense of self-esteem and exalted status among the "spirit people" amounts to a denial of authority. Their understanding of the freedom bestowed upon them by the Spirit calls into question God's will for specific patterns of roles, statuses, and orderly relationships on earth and in heaven. Paul argues that the pattern existing in heaven ought to be mirrored on earth. In the concluding verses (12-13), Paul declares that not only is the diversity of gifts among human beings unified in the same Spirit, but the diversity of ethnic groups (Israelites and non-Israelites) and roles (slaves or free persons) is similarly unified in the "one" Spirit. The gospel (John 20:19-23, or John 15:26-27; 16:12-15) describes yet other gifts of the Spirit (power to forgive and retain sins; guidance to all truth) intended to maintain unity in the community.

Trinity Sunday
2 Corinthians 13:11-13

These verses form the conclusion to that segment of Second Corinthians in which Paul has been rather harsh. This explains the imperatives: rejoice, mend your ways, encourage one another, agree with one another, live in peace. Despite the hard feelings toward his opponents in this community and the hard tone he has had to take with them, Paul desperately wants the divisions to end and harmonious fellowship to return. This indeed is his concluding prayer.

More than once in his letters, Paul recommends that believers greet one another with a holy kiss (1 Thess 5:26; 1 Cor 16:20; 2 Cor 13:13). Justin Martyr (ca. A.D. 100–165) reports this as part of the liturgy: "Having ended the prayers, we salute one another with a kiss" (*Apol.* 1.65.2). Perhaps Paul draws his recommendation from the liturgical setting. No doubt Westerners do not have to be reminded that in the ancient world and in other parts of the world even today, the "kiss" is extended by two people (including two men) who embrace, and then usually the younger or one of lower status will kiss the one of higher status on each cheek.

It is not clear what might make the kiss "holy." Perhaps Jesus' comment to Judas: "Judas, are you betraying the Son of Man with a kiss?" (Luke 22:48) offers some insight. In the honor-driven culture of the ancient Mediterranean world, betrayal or breach of loyalty is shocking enough. Expressing this disloyalty in non-verbal language (a kiss) whose primary purpose is to express respect and loyalty only compounds the perversion. Thus, perhaps the kiss during the liturgy is holy because by means of it believers express respect and loyalty to each other.

In today's gospel, John's Jesus says God wishes eternal life for those who believe in Jesus. Paul's wish for the Corinthian community is that they, too, should commit themselves with complete loyalty to Jesus, live in harmony, and thereby strengthen fellowship given by the Spirit resulting in union with the Spirit.

Eleventh Sunday
in Ordinary Time
Romans 5:6-11

[See Third Sunday of Lent for background comments about 5:1-2, 5-8 and this chapter's place in Romans.] In order to understand this text-segment, we need to reflect briefly on rites which include ritual and ceremony. The reason is that this text-segment reflects a judgment ritual. In general, ritual is the rite that human beings use to cross boundaries; for example, from the single state to the married state. Ceremony is the rite that human beings use to confirm a situation, such as the celebration of a wedding anniversary: dinner, champagne, exchange of cards, renewal of vows, and the like.

Thus rituals are irregular, unpredictable (use them when needed), move one from a present situation to future possibilities (man and woman to mother and father), are presided over by professionals (clergy person, lawyer, school president, etc.), and serve to reverse or transform status (e.g., single to married). Many rituals are stable ways of dealing with necessary instability in a system: the single people who marry rupture the fabric of their family of origin.

In contrast, ceremonies are quite regular (think of the wedding anniversary, birthday or name day), predictable and planned, move one from the present to a past event (one's marriage, one's day of birth, etc.), presided over by officials (the marriage partners, the parents of the child, etc.), and they serve to confirm roles and statuses in institutions (e.g., in kinship: parents and offspring, husband and wife, etc.).

Rituals produce status reversal or status transformation. These occasions pose risk to society, thus they require the assistance of professionals such as healers, prophets, and the like. Examples of status reversal or transformation would be the cleansing of sinners, admitting outsiders into the formerly exclusive "in-group," or bringing people on the periphery (like so-called lepers in the Bible) to the center (full-fledged members of the community again).

The key word in our text-segment is "reconciled," which Paul repeats three times. Sinners (called "enemies" in v. 10) who shame God should receive God's wrath! This is normal in an honor culture. Shame demands retaliation, and the most honorable God should retaliate. But the death of Jesus Messiah reconciled sinners to God, who in turn acquits them. Even more marvelous than that, acquitted sinners now have a share in the risen life of Jesus Messiah. They are restored to being friends of God. God graciously transforms the status of sinners to that of being justified.

Matthew's Jesus in today's gospel (9:36–10:8) takes pity on the crowd "because they were troubled and abandoned, like sheep without a shepherd." Jesus commissions twelve to minister to them by driving out unclean spirits and healing their ills. Exorcism and healing are rituals which transform status. Paul reminds his letter recipients that God and Jesus Messiah alone are capable of working the transformation required to enjoy authentic life to the full. Believers enculturated to be self-reliant would benefit by reflecting on that fact.

Twelfth Sunday in Ordinary Time
Romans 5:12-15

[Preachers and other readers must be careful not to impose on vv. 12- 14 the refined contemporary understanding of the dogma of Original Sin. While Trent (see Session V, 2–4, echoing the Sixteenth Council of Carthage [A.D. 418] and the Second Council of Carthage [A.D. 529]) said these verses do teach a form of the dogma, one must be fair to Paul who did not even use the phrase "original sin." That originated with Augustine. The reality of the sin and its universal terrible impact on all creation are a constant throughout history. Regarding other aspects of this notion, there were significant differences in the tradition.]

In this text-segment, we recognize a familiar thought pattern that recurs in the Pauline literature: then and now; the period of Adam, Sin, and Death; and the period of Jesus, righteousness, and life. Sin reigned from Adam until Jesus Messiah; Jesus' obedience ended that reign and inaugurated a new period of grace.

Sin and Death in these paragraphs are personifications. Sin is an active force within and among all human beings. As Paul notes, it has been present since the very beginnings of the human race. In the Israelite understanding, Sin expresses itself chiefly through the "flesh." Flesh is not a synonym for body but rather describes a person from the perspective of unredeemed weakness. Death is also a personified, cosmic force which has two effects: it destroys the human body and causes definitive separation from God. Thus for Paul, Sin is the twin of Death.

Paul's main interest is not Sin and Death but rather Adam and Jesus. He contrasts the two. The world was changed by each. Adam unleashed into the world an active hostile force (Sin) which had the power to cause definitive alienation from God (Death), the source of all life. The force (Sin) was accepted and ratified by all individuals who sinned through personal, actual misdeeds (v. 12). In contrast, Jesus's redemptive death unleashed uprightness and life for all who accept (believe in) him. The tragedy of Adam's failure is offset by the magnificent plenitude of Jesus' redemption.

The far-reaching perverse consequence of Adam's disobedience is reported according to a rabbinic model that divided time into three periods. The first extended from Adam to Moses during which time there was no law to disobey (v. 14). Still, Adam's transgression was so powerful that the death it caused (separation from God) dominated. All humanity during the period lived in Sin and subjection to Death. The second extended from Moses to the Messiah during which the law occasioned many transgressions. The third period, from the Messiah onward, brought the gracious gift of one, Jesus the Messiah, that resulted in acquittal, justification, but above all, life for all. Humanity in the image of the new Adam enjoys God's righteousness and "reigns in life."

Matthew's Jesus (10:26-33) exhorts the Twelve: "Fear no one!" The passive voice in the next verses (be revealed; be made known) is theological, that is, an indirect way of speaking of God without mentioning God's name. In a culture where secrecy, deception, and lying are customary, it is consoling to know that God speaks truth, God makes life right. Paul, too, is convinced that God through Jesus made sinful human beings righteous again. Thank God for God!

Thirteenth Sunday in Ordinary Time
Romans 6:3-4, 8-11

Paul's reflection on baptism in these verses describes a ritual that brings about a transformation of status. He is ever concerned about boundaries separating two spheres (e.g., life and death) and strategies for crossing these boundaries (e.g., baptism). This concern with boundaries flows from Paul's Pharisaic background. As such he was concerned with the holy, protecting and guarding it. Yet he acknowledges legitimate gates to approach the holy. Thus he identifies baptism as a ritual process determining who can legitimately cross the boundary to approach the holy.

Baptism brings outsiders legitimately into the realm of God. As a ritual process it has three stages: separation, liminality, and re-aggregation. Candidates are separated from their former world, whether Israelite or pagan, and its various practices including its alleged life of vice and allegiance to Satan and his kingdom (see Eph 4:17–5:20). In the liminal state, these candidates are as if in a "no-man's land." They are neither here nor there, separated from the old but not yet in the new. They are neither Jew nor Greek, slave nor free person, etc. (see Gal 3:28). The baptismal washing helps them cross that boundary. Legitimated by the ritual of baptism, these candidates may enter the holy temple of the church and are collected into God's society of kin and holy people.

Paul's favorite terms for discussing baptism and its effects are death/dying and rising to new life. These verses resound with this vocabulary. Candidates imitate the ritual of Jesus himself—his death, burial, and resurrection. They die to sin and death, descend into the tomb, are buried with Jesus, but rise with him to new life. To summarize, candidates for baptism leave one world, cross a boundary, and enter another world. The difference between the two worlds is expressed in vocabulary that describes the irreconcilable differences between the before and after states, that is, darkness and light.

Matthew's Jesus in today's gospel (Matt 10:37-42) invites his apostles to make a similar ritual crossing from one world to another, from one family (their family of origin) to another (the surrogate family established by Jesus). A follower of Jesus is always checking her or his location and making the required moves as needed.

Fourteenth Sunday in Ordinary Time
Romans 8:9, 11-13

Today we encounter another set of contrasting words that Paul likes to use in discussing the human condition: flesh and spirit. Flesh connotes natural, concretely material human existence. In these verses it is equivalent to slavery and suggests something outside of God's realm. Paul connects flesh with Death: "the concern of the flesh is death" (Rom 8:6). Moreover, "the concern of the flesh is hostility toward God; it does not submit to the law of God, nor can it; and those who are in the flesh cannot please God" (Rom 8:7-8). It is a rather depressing picture. In contrast, spirit denotes freedom and suggests things of God and heaven. It is the very power which raised Jesus' human and mortal body from death to holiness and life (Rom 8:10).

The Israelite tradition believed that human beings were pulled in two different directions or ways by different spirits: good ones and evil ones. Human beings are caught in the middle of a battle that never ends: in the heavens, on earth, and within the individual person. The question is: Which spirit will "lord" it over a person? The same is true of the on-going struggle between flesh and spirit. "For the flesh has desires against the Spirit, and the Spirit against the flesh" (Gal 5:17). Romans 8:1-17, which describes the workings of God's Spirit unto salvation, balances the preceding section (Rom 7:7-12) in which Paul describes himself at the mercy of a force that is not of God. From this perspective, the reader can sense and appreciate Paul's relief and the urgency with which he exhorts the letter recipients to live by the Spirit.

In today's gospel (Matt 11:25-30), Jesus acknowledges the gracious gifts of the Father which he in turn can share with others. In his own way, Paul attempts to share with his letter recipients the precious insights he has gained from "the one who raised Christ from the dead." Personal testimony to the workings of God in human life are a powerful witness to the weak and skeptical. But it must be more than simply telling one's story. To be truly helpful, it must be as insightful as Jesus' and Paul's testimonies.

Fifteenth Sunday
in Ordinary Time
Romans 8:18-23

Continuing his development of the idea that the believer's life is destined for singular and unimaginable honor (glory), Paul now explains how material creation is also included. Because of Adam's sin (Gen 3:15-17), material nature was cursed, subject to decay itself just like the human beings for whom it had been created. This solidarity in punishment also entails solidarity in redemption. So creation eagerly awaits and groans in labor pains until that final state of glory will be definitively restored.

This reflection has special cultural significance. In general, Mediterranean cultures of antiquity recognized that they had absolutely no control over material creation. They were subject to it; they had to suffer and endure it. Thus our ancestors in the faith believed that because of Adam's sin, human beings had no control over nature, yet the redemption of Adam would include the redemption of material creation as well.

What is the basis for Paul's confidence? He draws insight from the notion of first fruits of a harvest. When offered to God, these first fruits consecrated the entire harvest and became, as it were, down-payment, pledge, or guarantee of what was still to come. The Spirit serves this purpose for believers. Since the believer is already son/ child of God (Rom 8:15), the full implementation of this status will include the redemption of the body.

The imagery of the sower and seed in today's gospel (Matt 13:1-23) obviously relates to the notion of first fruits used by Paul to explain the fullness of glory humans patiently wait to attain. The combination of both readings helps the modern believer to expand awareness beyond the self, the human world, to the larger material world in which human beings live. Indeed, redemption has significance for the entire cosmos. As American business is wont to say, it is a good idea to think big!

Sixteenth Sunday in Ordinary Time
Romans 8:26-27

According to Paul, three things persuade us of the greatness of the glory or intimate share in God's life which is the destiny of each believer: the testimony of creation (vv. 19-22, see the preceding Sunday), the conviction of believers (vv. 23-25, preceding Sunday), and the testimony of the Spirit (vv. 26-30). In saying that "we do not know how to pray as we ought" (v. 26), Paul seems to contradict what he said just a few verses earlier, that the Spirit prompts us to pray with confidence: "Abba, my Father" (Rom 8:15). It is possible that Paul offers a corrective here to enthusiasm, namely, an exaggerated emphasis on the gifts of the Spirit. It is always possible to be overconfident. The truth is, of course, that because of natural human shortcomings, the Spirit adds its intercessions to our inadequate expressions. God knows this.

From a cultural perspective, it is important to notice Paul's indirect reference to God as "the one who searches hearts" (v. 27). Ancient Eastern Mediterranean culture was not only non-introspective but anti-introspective. Human beings have no ability at all to peer into the inner workings of themselves or others. They can judge only by externals. God alone reads hearts (see 1 Sam 16:7; 1 Kgs 8:39; also Pss 7:10; 17:3; 139:1). When the Gospels report that Jesus knew what others were thinking (e.g., Mark 2:8), the evangelists are presenting Jesus as an extraordinary human being who does something only

God can do. For the evangelist's Mediterranean audience this was more impressive than working mighty deeds which, as Jesus himself intimated, many of their own kin were able to do (see Matt 11:27). In the West, of course, psychology has a status close to religion, and people in Western cultures in general feel quite confident they can know what others are thinking and what it all means. This is a major difference between ourselves and our ancestors in the faith, one that is evident throughout the Bible.

Speaking in parables as Jesus does in today's gospel (Matt 13:24-43) is also an indirect way of speaking about God. Westerners who live in a low-context culture, one that expects everything to be spelled out in explicit detail, are understandably puzzled by the statements of Jesus and Paul who lived in high-context cultures. High context cultures presume that all conversation partners know how to supply what is assumed in all conversations. Perhaps this helps explain the important role of the Spirit in that context. It's not that God wouldn't know all the details, but God might like to hear them, and the Spirit can supply whatever humans have taken for granted.

Seventeenth Sunday in Ordinary Time
Romans 8:28-30

Scholars caution against reading into these verses later, and specifically Augustinian, notions of predestination of individuals to eternal bliss or to eternal damnation. Two key points help to understand that this is not Paul's meaning. One, the English word "purpose" translates Paul's Greek, *prothesis,* which has the idea of a plan, especially one made in advance. And what is God's plan? To bring all who have responded to God's initiative with love to salvation, to eternal bliss. Everything in creation is an object of God's love, beneficence, and good will (see Eph 1:5).

Paul spells out the plan clearly. Those who respond to God's call must progressively conform themselves to Jesus by a gradually increasing participation in his risen life. What stands out in Paul's understanding of God's plan is God's initiative: in everything God works for good with those who love God. God is the one who calls, justifies, and glorifies. These are beyond human merit or effort, though human beings have a choice in accepting or rejecting the call.

The second key element is to carefully note all the plurals in these verses. Paul, a collectivistic personality living in a collectivistic culture, can only think in terms of the collectivity. Individuals derive meaning and fulfillment in life from their total embeddedness in the collectivity. Thus, the collectivity that loves God is the one that will benefit from God's plan.

In today's gospel (Matt 13:44-52), Jesus tells the parable of the net which collects all kinds of fish, the good and the bad. Bad fish could be those prohibited by Leviticus (11:9-12) or fish that have died and are decomposing. If the latter interpretation is more plausible, it links well with Paul's reflection that God wills the welfare and salvation of all creatures, but some may have preferred death to life.

Eighteenth Sunday in Ordinary Time
Romans 8:35, 37-39

As Paul brings his reflection on Christian life to a close in this chapter of Romans, he insists that nothing can separate us from the love that Jesus (v. 35) or God (v. 39) has for us, which was made so evident in the death and resurrection of Jesus.

To explain "nothing" Paul lists two major sources of threat: earthly and cosmic. He lists seven earthly threats which signal that Paul is using a topos, that is, a statement of exhortation on a particular topic (e.g., Rom 13:1-7 on duty to the state; Rom 14:1-23 on eating certain foods; etc.) usually presented in a conventional form. In other words, to try to identify with specificity the meaning of each word would be rather futile. A topos is equivalent to simply saying: "let me give you some examples," but the examples are not necessarily carefully thought out and shaded in nuance. In general, however, each of these seven items is a shameful experience. In a culture driven by the core value of honor, people are obliged to avoid shame because of its social consequences. Here Paul says even the social consequences of these shameful experiences will not drive us away from fidelity to Jesus or God.

The second major source is even more frightening, since it involves astral beings who exert a powerful influence upon human beings and the earth. Indeed, they wage war on God's creatures. Like all people in his culture (including Jesus),

Paul was convinced that human beings were involved in a war with malevolent cosmic powers out to destroy them. Those who lived at Qumran wrote: "All their punishments and their periods of grief [i.e., the sons of justice] are caused by the dominion of his [i.e., the Angel of Darkness] enmity. And all the spirits of their lot cause the sons of light to fail. However, the God of Israel and the angel of his truth assist all the sons of light" (1QS 3:23-25).

In v. 38 Paul names some of these malevolent cosmic beings: principalities *(archai),* powers *(dynameis).* He repeats these and adds others elsewhere in his letters: dominations or authorities *(exousiai)* and lordships (*kyriotetes;* see 1 Cor 15:24; Col 1:16; 2:10, 15; Eph 1:21; 6:12). In ancient astrological lore, these are the decans, astral deities that dominate over every ten *(deka)* degrees of the circle of the Zodiac. When these were absorbed into the Israelite-based Christian tradition, they became "elders" around the throne of God (e.g., Rev 4:10). The angels Paul mentions are in this context malevolent angels. Risen Jesus Messiah now holds preeminence over all of these beings (Col 1:16).

In today's gospel (Matt 14:13-21), Jesus rescued more than five thousand hungry people by feeding them. Paul tells us the Risen Jesus has rescued human beings from cosmic beings as well. He has destroyed every Rule, Authority, and Power (1 Cor 15:24). The final victory, however, remains to be won as Paul notes at the end of Romans: "The God of Peace will quickly crush Satan under your feet" (16:20). Yet the war is still going on, and until the end Satan remains a deadly foe. Paul's words in today's reading remind us of what has already been accomplished to our great benefit. Let us not give that up too easily.

Nineteenth Sunday in Ordinary Time
Romans 9:1-5

In Romans 9–11, Paul draws heavily on the Hebrew Bible to explain how God's resolve to "include" non-Israelites in the chosen community seems to have ironically "excluded" the very people who were initially chosen to form this community. These first five verses express Paul's anguish that the majority of his Israelite sisters and brothers (v. 3, using their God-given title, see Gen 32:38-39) have failed to come to faith in the gospel and thus inherit the promises God made to them long ago. Then, in another conventional form (see "topos" in the reflection for the Eighteenth Sunday in Ordinary Time, above), Paul lists seven prerogatives of Israelites to which he adds an eighth: the Messiah.

Several cultural considerations sharpen our understanding of these introductory verses. One, Paul's insistence that he does not lie but speaks the truth in the Messiah (v. 1). Secrecy, deception, and lying are acceptable strategies for preserving one's reputation in this culture. People routinely expect it and always wonder whether or not to believe what the speaker is saying. When a speaker wants to assure the listener that truth indeed is being told, the speaker usually utters an oath ("I speak the truth in Christ") or curses himself if the statement is not the complete truth ("I wish I myself were accursed"). Paul is truly grieved about fellow Israelites who have not accepted Jesus as God's Messiah. He takes no pleasure in this knowledge.

A second consideration is Paul's conscience. We would be mistaken to understand it as we understand conscience in the modern, Western world, namely, as internalized rules or an internal police officer monitoring and assuring proper individual behavior. In Paul's anti-introspective culture, conscience is knowledge shared with others in a social group, common awareness. In Paul's group-oriented or collectivistic society, conscience represents the advice, customs, norms, praise, and censure of fellow human beings with whom one lives. The purpose of this common knowledge is to keep the family, group, village, everybody sound, both corporately and socially. Paul's corporate group is "my own people, my kindred according to the flesh" (v. 3), and both their behavior and resolve to reject Jesus as Messiah has torn the group apart, causing him sorrow and anguish.

A third cultural consideration is the notion of "curse" (Greek: *anathema*). To curse, declare anathema, or expel someone from the community is an exit ritual. In all his letters, Paul is concerned about boundaries: who should be in and who should be thrown out (see e.g., 1 Cor 5:2). For a collectivistic personality to be thrown out of the group is equivalent to a death sentence. That Paul wishes this for himself if it would help rescue his "own people" demonstrates not only the depth of his grief but the seriousness with which he considers the alienation of his "kindred according to the flesh."

Today's gospel (Matt 14:22-33) reports a group experience in an altered state of consciousness of Jesus walking on the sea. While Jesus chides Peter (in the singular) for his little faith, nothing in the report indicates that the eleven differed from Peter in this matter. Peter the collectivistic personality was not aided by the group on this occasion. Paul the collectivistic personality is pained by his group. While no one would suggest individualists trade their cultural values for collectivistic ones, individuals are always challenged to raise their sensitivity to group problems.

Twentieth Sunday in Ordinary Time
Romans 11:13-15, 29-32

At this point in the letter, Paul turns his attention specifically to non-Israelites and speaks to them as "the apostle to the Gentiles." His major point in chapter 11 is that Israel's disbelief is only partial and temporary. The concluding verse sums up his thinking. God wants to show mercy to all people, Israelites and non-Israelites alike. God's plan then was to deliver all to disobedience so that God might show mercy to all.

Paul's comment about making his people jealous is perfectly intelligible in the Mediterranean world. A mother or father will sometimes take a toy from one child and give it to another precisely in order to make one jealous of the other, but more importantly to make the deprived child more attentive to the respective parent. When that happens, the parent will reward the child from whom the toy was originally withdrawn.

God's gifts and call are irrevocable. Israel is still eligible to receive mercy. Speaking to non-Israelites, Paul reasons thus. Just as you were once disobedient and God showed you mercy because of Israelite disobedience, so Israel's disobedience may also result in mercy from God since God has given it to you in a similar situation. Thus just as Romans 1–8 highlighted the inclusion of the non-Israelites in the gospel, now Romans 9–11 highlights the inclusion of Israelites in the same gospel.

Matthew's Jesus depicted in today's gospel (Matt 15:21-28) was very much an in-group person having no interest in or regard for out-group members (Canaanite woman). In the game of challenge and riposte, which she by gender and ethnicity was not even qualified to play, the woman beats Jesus and forces him to be "inclusive" at least on this occasion. Paul tells us that inclusivity has been God's plan all along, but he too uses a cultural device (jealousy) to implement it. What cultural strategies might modern, Western believers pursue to implement God's plan for mercy for all?

Twenty-First Sunday in Ordinary Time
Romans 11:33-36

Having completed to his satisfaction a reflection upon how Israel fits into God's plans for salvation and redemption, Paul concludes with a brief and impressively constructed hymn of praise to the all-merciful God. The apostle has absolutely no doubt that God has complete control over history and human life. God alone knows its design, purpose, and fulfillment. The insight that leads Paul to formulate this prayer is his understanding of how Israelites and non-Israelites end up assisting one another in the attainment of salvation.

How could anyone understand or explain this? Paul draws on the Israelite scriptural tradition to shed some light. No one has advised God (Isa 40:13), nor is God in debt to anyone (probably the Targum on Job 41:3a). God is the creator, sustainer, and goal of the universe (v. 36). These ideas are very likely derived from Stoicism as it was accepted by Hellenistic Judaism and absorbed by Paul in his education, travels, and experience. God alone is responsible for the origin, course, and purpose of the universe. To God be honor (= glory) forever. Amen.

When, in today's gospel (Matt 16:13-20), Peter says to Jesus: "You are the Messiah, the Son of the living God," Jesus observes that only the Father could have given him this insight. So too does Paul realize that only God could have come up with such a plan to show mercy to Israelites and non-Israelites, for which Paul gives honor (= glory) to God. How do modern believers get insights and glimpses into God's view of things?

Twenty-Second Sunday in Ordinary Time
Romans 12:1-2

As in other letters, so too here Paul concludes with practical exhortations. Romans 12–13 spell them out in general, while Romans 14–15 deal with a situation involving the relationship between those who are "weak" in faith with those who are "strong" in faith. In general, the idea is that Christian freedom should promote life in peace and harmony among all believers.

These first two verses make three appeals. (1) The letter recipients ought to offer themselves ("your bodies" [v. 1]) as a living sacrifice to God. (2) They ought not reflect their culture ("do not conform yourselves to this age" [v. 2]), but rather shape it. (3) They ought to let God transform them.

The first appeal hearkens back to the beginning of this letter (Rom 1:18–3:20) where Paul lamented the unfortunate human condition without Jesus Messiah. People did not behave according to God's plan. Specifically, pagans "revered and worshiped the creature rather than the creator" (Rom 1:25). Since they failed to acknowledge God, "God handed them over to their undiscerning mind to do what is improper" (Rom 1:28). Their determination resulted in a culturally disapproved treatment of the human body (Rom 1:24, 26-27). Offering oneself (your bodies) as a "living sacrifice" to God contrasts starkly with animal sacrifices unaccompanied by true change of heart (1 Sam 15:22; Isa 1:10-20; etc.).

The second challenge calls for the letter-recipients to learn the art of discernment. The practices criticized by Paul in Rom 1:18–3:20 were not even condoned by their culture! Hence Paul's exhortation that they should strive to discern God's will and obey it. This is a constant concern in all of Paul's letter. All should learn God's will (Rom 2:18) and do it (Rom 12:2). "The will of God is your sanctification" (1 Thess 4:3). The third challenge is to allow God to work in their lives and transform them so they might do what is good and pleasing and perfect.

Some scholars have suggested a different translation for "spiritual worship" (v. 1): "the worship you owe as rational beings." "Spiritual" has the sense of "inward," in contrast to the external, physical, and material. This would seem to agree with Paul's implicit contrast with material sacrifices familiar from Temple worship. But since Paul here lays new emphasis on the bodily aspect of new Christian worship, "rational"—the element that distinguishes human beings—seems preferable, particularly as Paul calls for renewal of mind and rational discernment in the next verse.

In today's gospel (Matt 16:21-27), Jesus presents instruction in terms of reversal (lose life yet save it). This instruction was a common motif in the ancient world. In the *Anabasis,* Xenophon said this to inspire young men to go to war. Jesus' message, however, is directed to a higher level. With proper discernment, a believer would gain life eternal (not just a plaque or medal for dying in war) by knowing how to lose life. This is the kind of discernment of God's will that Paul encourages. Here is a skill that requires great effort to attain, but its acquisition pays rich life-dividends.

Twenty-Third Sunday in Ordinary Time
Romans 13:8-10

Simple as the words of these verses are, Western readers will miss Paul's point if they interpret "love" as referring to feelings of affection, sentiments of fondness, or warm, glowing affinity as is the case in Western culture. The primary value orientation of Paul's cultural world was a concern for the group as superior to the individual. Thus horizontal relationships are important: concern for kin, for knowing who is one's neighbor, for the common good of the in-group, and loving the in-group neighbor. This is unmistakably clear in Lev 19:17-18, where neighbor is one's fellow ethnic, one's brother. It is noteworthy that Paul cites this text (v. 9) with no explicit reference to the Jesus tradition (Matt 22:34-40; Mark 12:28-34; Luke 10:25-28).

Love in this cultural context means group attachment and group bonding. Such love puts the group first, with maximum effort directed toward maintaining group integrity. Paul's exhortation at this point in this letter is a natural follow-up from what he just wrote a few verses earlier: "Love one another with mutual affection; anticipate one another in showing honor" (Rom 12:10). It is also a smooth introduction to the next section (Romans 13–14) in which he will reflect on divisive behaviors by those "strong" in the faith to the detriment of those "weak" in the faith.

Paul cites some of the commandments as concrete illustrations of behavior that harm one's neighbor and would certainly divide a community. Such behaviors do not spring from love understood as group attachment and group integrity. Commentators point out that Paul does not cite the commandments as they are found in Exod 20:13-17 and Deut 5:17-21. Josephus gives the reason: "It is not lawful for us to set [these precepts] down directly, but their import we will declare" (*Antiquities* 3.5.4; Whiston translation). In other words, the list of commandments, like the sacred name of God (YHWH), was not to be recited or stated directly in the order found in the Torah.

In today's gospel (Matt 18:15-20), Matthew's Jesus presents a program of conflict resolution, to use a modern term, for use in a community of believers. He explains how to deal with someone who refuses to pay his debt of "love" to another. Paul's concluding phrase is the model to follow: "Love does no evil to the neighbor." Keeping the group perspective in mind in all discussions of love will be the major challenge for the modern individualistically oriented believer. It is, however, an emphasis that provides a healthy balance to the value of individualism.

Twenty-Fourth Sunday in Ordinary Time
Romans 14:7-9

These verses are carved from a larger unit (Romans 14–15) in which Paul exhorts the community to tolerance. Paul specifically discourages ridicule of and passing judgment on others who think and behave differently (Rom 14:3 and 10). Paul offers one more reason in these verses: Jesus is Lord of all. The symmetrical structure of these verses suggest that they may have been a hymn or statement of faith which had previously been composed and repeated in communities of believers. While Paul's advice is a commonplace of conventional wisdom in the ancient world ("no one lives or ought to live for self alone"), he adds a distinctive note to it with the mention of death. By his death and resurrection, Jesus gained lordship over life and death. In baptism, believers have died to all other "lords" and accepted Jesus as the only Lord. This means that all dimensions of human life including death are subsumed in the relationship to the Lord.

In the gospel (Matt 18:21-35), Jesus presents God as a model of forgiveness that humans ought to imitate. Paul's instruction to his letter recipients is something of a variation of this lesson. The offended human being must look beyond self and seeking satisfaction. Someone else is Lord and will see to the needs of those who acknowledge that lordship. Believers culturally oriented toward self-sufficiency and being in charge will find this a challenging but rewarding lesson to learn. Yet again, the community stands to benefit.

Twenty-Fifth Sunday in Ordinary Time
Philippians 1:20c-24, 27a

[For introductory comments, see Palm Sunday, above.] Today we begin a series of readings from Letter B (from prison in Rome) to the Philippians. Yanked from their literary, historical, and cultural context, these verses can be read by anyone anywhere and contribute to a splendid ethnocentric meditation, perhaps even a sermon. Consider this historical scenario as one plausible context for understanding the present verses respectfully in their historical context. In 1 Thessalonians, the first of Paul's surviving and collected letters and the oldest document in the New Testament, we get the impression that Paul may not have expected to die before the return of Jesus (1 Thess 4:15). He repeats this conviction to the Corinthians: "We shall not all fall asleep, but we shall all be changed" (1 Cor 15:51). But a short while later, Paul tells the Corinthians about his experience in Ephesus: "We were utterly weighed down beyond our strength, so that we despaired even of life. Indeed, we had accepted within ourselves the sentence of death" (2 Cor 1:8-9). Scholars are not agreed on what brought Paul to this experience, but it could plausibly have been something like the riot stirred by Demetrius and the silversmiths in Ephesus (Acts 19:23-41). In other words, Paul initially believed he would be alive at the Second Coming. Some crisis brought him close to death and the realization that he would probably die before the Second Coming.

In this context, today's verses reflect this latter conviction. Paul is in prison as he writes this letter, and his life is literally on the line. The Emperor's judgment could be to execute him. Paul muses about how much he would like to be with Christ (that is, dead), yet if he continues to live the Philippians and others will continue to benefit from his ministry. In the broader context of these verses (1:27–2:18), Paul uses vocabulary concerning citizenship and military experience to encourage these Philippian believers to choose what is best despite conflicting messages from non-Christian neighbors or fellow believers. The phrase "conduct yourselves" is citizenship language. Literally it is "live as a citizen," and Paul qualifies it with "worthy of the gospel." Effectively it means, since you know the responsibilities your Roman citizenship implies, apply the same rules of conduct in your relationship with Jesus and the gospel which should be the focus of your higher allegiance. If you suffer for it, no matter. All suffering, just like Paul's, contributes to promoting the gospel.

Today's gospel (Matthew 20:1-16a) presents the behavior of God under the image of a Mediterranean patron. A patron has freedom to choose his clients and to treat them as if they were blood kin. The treatment, of course, is great, but it is always at the discretion of the patron. Paul speaks of God in the same way. God can choose to keep Paul alive or take him to eternal life. It really isn't Paul's choice. What is important is to conduct oneself "in a way worthy of the gospel of Christ." The advice is still sound today.

Twenty-Sixth Sunday in Ordinary Time
Philippians 2:1-11

As we continue our reading from Paul's letter to the Philippians, he tells this community what would make his joy complete. He lists a series of qualities that should characterize a person who lives "in Christ." This latter phrase occurs 165 times in the Pauline letters with several meanings. Most commonly it describes the close, life-giving and life-impacting union between Jesus and a believer who are united in a symbiotic relationship. Such an intimate union should have concrete results. This indeed is what Paul lists.

Above all, Paul emphasizes the importance of "being of the same mind, with the same love, united in heart, thinking one thing" (v. 2). Such advice is pertinent to a community like this one plagued by internal squabbles about how one properly should live "in Christ." He follows with concrete instructions for behavior (vv. 3-4): don't act from a motive of selfishness or vainglory but humbly consider others as more important and look out for the interests of others. This advice is quite in line with what one would expect of collectivistic personalities living in a collectivistic culture. Collectivistic personalities always behave for the benefit of the group and do not see their own personal fulfillment.

Two pieces of cultural background help to understand these verses. First, Paul singles out two of the three symbolic body zones and urges that believers keep them in harmony.

Hands-feet (instructions for behavior) should follow the dictates of heart-eyes (think one and the same thing; agree on proper behavior). Second, Paul draws on the common cultural understanding of "humility" as the motivating factor. In Paul's world, humility means not creating the impression of overstepping one's rightful place, of impinging on others. Hence, "regard others as more important than yourselves." This is important because as Paul continues, he cites a hymn illustrating the humiliation of Jesus but with a twist (for an explanation of this hymn, see Palm Sunday, above).

A second consideration is to keep in mind that Philippi was a Roman colony most of whose citizens were retired from the military. They had strong ties to Rome and would be quite willing to participate in the imperial cult that acknowledged Caesar as divine. It is therefore plausible that Paul is vigorously arguing against such participation. His use of certain words (Lord), proposed gestures (bending the knee), mention of an empire (Phil 2:10), and the acclamation "Jesus is Lord" all echo the language of the imperial cult but speak instead of Jesus. Paul is deliberately commanding the Philippians to acknowledge Jesus as Lord rather than Caesar, who at this time is very likely Nero. This, however, is a treasonous act. What course of action would a retired military person who is devoted to Rome but believes in Jesus choose?

Moreover, the emphasis on unity in vv. 1-5 reflects the unity that should characterize a Roman colony. Paul uses a topos on unity from ancient political rhetoric to strengthen his exhortation. (A topos is a statement of exhortation on a particular topic [e.g., Rom 13:1-7 on duty to the state; Rom 14:1-23 on eating certain foods; etc.] usually presented in a conventional form.) For Paul, concord is not only a civic responsibility but a Christian responsibility. Thus "selfishness and conceit" (v. 3) are a signal of offenses against harmonious community life, probably along party lines as in Corinth (1 Corinthians 11) or Rome (Phil 1:14-18).

In today's gospel (Matt 21:28-32), Jesus focuses on something his Middle Eastern audience would tend to overlook: the fact that the shameless son who later felt ashamed of his behavior went and did his father's bidding after all. Paul hopes that his exhortation to humility will similarly make the Philippians ashamed of their bickering and seek to close ranks and live harmoniously.

Twenty-Seventh Sunday in Ordinary Time
Philippians 4:6-9

Nothing so disturbs a community as divisions, disagreement, and an undercurrent of dissent. The context of Letter B is precisely this, so in conclusion Paul exhorts the community to put away all anxiety and trust in God who will grant peace and equanimity beyond their wildest imaginations.

Verses 8 and 9 are a list of "virtues" that believers should imitate. Vice and virtue lists were very familiar in the Hellenistic world. Greco-Roman philosophers often began their speeches with a list of vices to depict the depravity from which they hoped to lift the masses by their instruction and guidance. While Paul's list, and particularly the one here, may have been inspired by those popular in late Stoicism, there are many significant differences. Regarding the form, pagan lists of proper conduct were often based on the cardinal virtues or the various parts of the soul. There is nothing like this in the New Testament; the word "virtue" is rare. (The Greek word that appears here in v. 8 is correctly translated "praise" not "virtue.") Paul's lists tend rather to be based on the aspects of human existence known as "flesh" and "spirit."

As for content, Paul's lists tend to be brief, and nearly all the so-called "virtues" he enumerates can be reduced to one word: agape, love, and its most obvious expressions: goodness, mercy, forgiveness, etc. Of special significance, however, is the advice in 4:8: "Think about these things!" The Greek verb for "think" is not the one Paul usually uses. This one means rather to take carefully into account, to calculate, to evaluate carefully. Paul is not condemning the society they live in. Actually, he acknowledges that much in that world is good (v. 8). Rather, he asks them to evaluate all options facing them and choose the best to do (just as he did in 1:9-10).

The purpose of these lists in general and in today's verses is the maintenance and strengthening of group cohesion. They are directed to members of the group to help it avoid inner-group antagonisms and group dissolution. They are not universalizing, nor even remotely concerned with individual spiritual development, growth in holiness, etc. Sanctions against violators come from community control (see 1 Cor 5:3; Deut 21:18-21).

Addressing his parable in today's gospel (Matt 21:33-43) to the chief priests and elders, Jesus warns that if they do not heed the Good News and produce its fruit, "the kingdom of God will be taken away from you and given to a people that will." Paul's variation on this message for the Philippians is to present a list of God-pleasing characteristics they should adopt. In the final analysis, Paul presents himself as a living example: "Keep on doing what you have learned and received and heard and seen in me" (v. 9; see also 3:17). This will bring peace to the divided community. It was common for teachers to exhort disciples to imitate and share in their striving for perfection. How powerful it would be if every member of the community could repeat Paul's confident saying to all the others.

Twenty-Eighth Sunday in Ordinary Time
Philippians 4:12-14, 19-20

Today's verses are the only ones in the three-year lectionary drawn from Letter A to the Philippians (Phil 4:10-20). Essentially this is a note sent by Paul to acknowledge receipt of the financial aid brought to him from the community by Epaphroditus. It has all the vocabulary and marks of similar commercial receipts common in this time and place. With regard to the Philippians, this note is a current reckoning of their ongoing account with Paul. This letter was written early in Paul's imprisonment. Some think that this is the situation to which he refers in 2 Cor 1:8.

Though some commentators call these verses part of a "thank you note," such a designation is ethnocentric. In the Middle East, to say thank you is to terminate a relationship. Effectively it says: "I won't be needing you any more." Recall that the Samaritan leper said thank you to Jesus because he considered it a stroke of great luck for himself, a Samaritan, to run into an Israelite who was gracious to him. It would be beyond his wildest dream that such an encounter would ever occur again. The other nine fellow Judeans would want to return to Jesus where their illness returned, as it very likely did (Luke 17:11-19). They would be fools to signal that they no longer needed or intended to have recourse to Jesus. Paul loves the Philippians and most certainly does not want to terminate his relationship with them. Prior to this they had already twice sent money to Paul while he was staying in Thessalonica.

There is a second element to this idea summed up in the Arab proverb: "Don't thank me, you will repay me." In the Middle East, a favor received is a favor owed. There are no "free" gifts because nothing is free. Everything requires a return. Accepting an invitation to dinner demonstrates the ability and willingness to repay at some future time with a return invitation. People unable to repay won't accept the invitation. Accepting healing from Jesus required that the recipient spread the news and enhance Jesus' reputation (= honor) far and wide.

Thus, Paul explains how life-experience has taught him how to live with abundance or with need, with enough to eat or going hungry. Further, while Paul doesn't say thank you (to the puzzlement of Western interpreters), he does acknowledge with appreciation the benevolence of his friends. "It was kind of you to share in my distress."

However, since he is in prison with no knowledge of when he will be released (which could indicate that he didn't even have sufficient funds to bribe his way out—which is the meaning of Matt 5:26), he is painfully aware that he may be unable to repay the favor as culture requires. Perhaps he wasn't able to repay the previous two gifts either. Thus his concluding prayer: "My God [on my behalf] will fully supply whatever you need, in accord with his glorious riches in Messiah Jesus."

Today's gospel (Matt 22:1-14) is based on the same cultural principles. The guests refuse an invitation, but as the story continues their refusal does not seem based on an inability to reciprocate. The king then invites people who are unable to reciprocate: a shocking scenario indeed! Since the parable is about God, and everything human beings know and say about God is based on human experience culturally conditioned, God's behavior runs contrary to the culture. That may be good news for some but bad news for others. Paul has covered himself well. Since he cannot personally repay the kindness of the Philippians, he trusts that God, his patron, will do it for him.

Twenty-Ninth Sunday in Ordinary Time

1 Thessalonians 1:1-5b

This earliest of all the New Testament documents (ca. A.D. 50) is also our introduction to Paul. We meet him and his companions for the first time approximately twenty years after Paul accepted Jesus as Messiah. Scholars think two letters have been combined into one. (Letter A = 2:13–4:2 written from Athens; and B = 1:1–2:12 and 4:3–5:28 written from Corinth). Today's reading is drawn from that standard part of the ancient letter called the letter-opening. While modern letter writers usually don't identify themselves until their signature at the end, ancient letter writers began by identifying themselves and the recipients, and then they send extended greetings to the recipients.

Three people are sending this letter. Silvanus (Greek: Silas) was a key member, prophet in, and ambassador on behalf of the Jerusalem Church (see Acts 15:22). That Church sent him to Antioch, Syria, and Cilicia to communicate the decision that Gentiles did not have to be circumcised in order to join the believing community. After his fall-out with Barnabas (Acts 15:36-39), Paul selected Silvanus to be his companion in subsequent mission work. One can safely assume that they had a warm bond of friendship.

Timothy was a fellow worker and trusted emissary of Paul mentioned in many letters (1 Thessalonians; 2 Corinthians; Philippians; Philemon; 2 Thessalonians; Colossians). Though he was the son of a Judaic mother and Greek father, Timothy was not circumcised (Acts 16:3). Quite likely, the Judaic traditions were not strictly observed in his home as he grew up. Paul refers to him as "our brother" and "God's fellow-worker in the gospel of Christ" (1 Thess 3:2). The two had a close relationship and were partners in evangelization.

To an eye trained to perceive aspects of Mediterranean culture, these references highlight Paul and his colleagues as collectivistic personalities. This kind of personality is represented among 80 percent of the contemporary world's population. It stands in stark contrast to individualism. Collectivisitic personalities need others to help develop and maintain their personal and group identity. By birth they are embedded in a very specific primary in-group. Thus they gain their basic identities from the family. Role and status flow from group expectations, whether this be the family or the surrogate family like the developing Messianist group with whom all three were associated. In other words, this Mediterranean trio needed each other for much more than moral support and encouragement.

The nature of collectivistic personalities helps us to understand what Paul praises among Thessalonian believers. They were chosen by God, therefore they should respond obediently. And this they did. The trio praises the Thessalonian believers for their "work of faith [= loyalty, faithfulness] and labor of love [= group allegiance and cohesion], and endurance in hope [= trust] rooted in our Lord, Jesus the Messiah" (v. 3). Loyalty, group allegiance, and trust require endurance, acceptance of suffering, maintaining the status quo, contentment. There is no thought of getting ahead or improving one's lot. Such behavior would be disruptive to the group.

Obedience is closely joined with endurance. Since the gospel came to you "in power and in the Holy Spirit and with much conviction," accept it, assent to it, embrace it, and live accordingly. Endure whatever gospel life brings in its wake. This is God's will.

What kind of bond exists between modern Christian leaders and the communities they lead or visit? Are gathering places filled to capacity when leaders visit, or is it difficult to encourage attendance for visiting evangelizers? What did our collectivistic ancestors in the faith have at their disposal that their modern individualists lack? Is there any way to compensate?

Thirtieth Sunday in Ordinary Time
1 Thessalonians 1:5c-10

Two distinct, Mediterranean cultural values stand out in this reading: the honorable status of suffering and the praiseworthy imitation of honorable behavior manifested by honorable people. While the Thessalonians may have known "what sort of people we [Paul, Silas, Timothy] were among you for your sake," we do not. The puzzle is all the greater when in the next breath there is mention of Thessalonians receiving the word "in great affliction." Were they in some kind of distress when they heard the good news? Did the good news bring suffering to them in its wake? Did the good news console them in some trouble?

We know, in general, that men in the Mediterranean world prove their manliness by enduring pain and suffering without flinching or complaining. It is indeed a model to imitate (see the model in 2 Maccabees 6, especially v. 28; and the imitation in 2 Maccabees 7). Apparently, the "brothers" in Thessalonika did this, perhaps imitating Paul, Silas, and Timothy in some way. The Thessalonians, in turn, became a model for all the believers in other parts of Greece (Macedonia and in Achaia). This is very honorable male behavior, hence the letter's authors pay a very high compliment to the letter's recipients.

But what of the women? What kind of suffering would women encounter receiving the word? We are as little informed about this as we are about the suffering of the men. News of the suffering, however—both men's and women's—would circulate. That suffering would certainly become a model for hearers of each gender. Yet, while the suffering of women is no less real than the suffering of men, its endurance does not have the same meaning in the Mediterranean world as the suffering of men. Suffering does not define a woman in the Mediterranean world in the same way it defines men.

Finally, Murphy-O'Connor highlights a problem that might have been caused by vv. 9b-10. The contrast between "wait for his son" and "Jesus who delivers us" is a contrast between a future event and a present one. Some think Jesus is yet to come, and others think Jesus has already returned to their midst. Those who embrace the latter opinion would be tempted to quit working (1 Thess 4:11) or worry about the fate of those who have already died (1 Thess 4:13). In technical jargon, this is the contrast between "future eschatology" and "realized eschatology." The topic will come up again in subsequent selections from Thessalonians.

The contemporary Western believer is faced with some serious challenges. How do believers in a presumably egalitarian and inclusive culture imitate their ancestors in the faith situated in the gender-divided, predominantly non-egalitarian, non-inclusive Mediterranean culture? How do contemporary men and women suffer with regard to the gospel, and how can that be imitated? Similarly in current Christian thinking, what is already present and what is still to come? Perhaps we speak too glibly about these matters without paying due attention to the very different situation of our ancestors. Translating this across millennia and across cultures is a huge challenge.

Thirty-First Sunday in Ordinary Time
1 Thessalonians 2:7b-9, 13

The three men who sent this letter (Paul, Silvanus, and Timothy) reveal an interesting dimension of Middle Eastern culture in these verses. To express the depth of their love and commitment to this community which they treated with gentleness and not with force, the men draw on the image of a wet-nurse. In the Middle East, young boys are raised together with young girls by all the women—the mother, her sisters if they are close by, the older female children—among other females who share the task of nurturing the children. Adult men are minimally involved, and the young boy doesn't come into more direct and regular contact with adult men until the age of puberty when he must move from the women's world into the men's world. Boys then spend a good deal of their adult years learning how to be a man.

This cultural tradition helps explain some images which modern, Western readers might find surprising. Paul compares himself to a wet nurse (v. 8) and to a mother in birth pains (Gal 4:19). Jesus compares himself to a mother-hen (Matt 23:37; Luke 13:34). Mediterranean men seem to draw on such female images spontaneously. It is this background that helps understand why the three apostles believed they shared their very lives (lectionary: selves) with the Thessalonians by preaching the gospel of God to them.

Yet another significant word appears in v. 13: "receiving the word of God from hearing us." The Greek term translated as "receiving" is a technical term sometimes used in conjunction with "handing on" (see 1 Cor 15:1-3). The terms indicate that the preacher or teacher is transmitting reliable tradition, perhaps verbatim, which the audience accepts and receives as such. It is not personal opinion or interpretation. It is not subject to debate. It is rather a statement of belief shaped and preserved in the community. The reward for obedient reception is that that word "is now at work in you who believe."

In the gospel (Matt 23:1-12), Jesus notes that those responsible for maintaining the tradition (scribes and Pharisees) know it well and teach it reliably. Unfortunately, they do not give a good example. "They preach but they do not practice." A stark contrast with the apostles who preach to the Thessalonians.

Thirty-Second Sunday in Ordinary Time
1 Thessalonians 4:13-18

Even as late as twenty years after Jesus died and was raised (the time when this letter was written), believers were expecting Jesus to return very soon, within their own lifetime. As loved ones began to die, and Jesus still had not returned, the surviving believers became very concerned. Paul addresses this concern in these verses. He begins (v. 14) with another early Christian statement of belief, a mini-creed as it were: "we believe that Jesus died and rose." In the same breath, Paul states the implication of this belief: so too will God bring with Jesus those who have died in him. This is a firm basis for hope.

Next Paul offers an insight based on "the word of the Lord," that is, a tradition from early Messianist prophecy understood as the will of God for the here and now. Notice that Paul himself still believes that he will be alive when the Lord returns ("we who are alive . . . until the coming of the Lord"). In other words, Paul thinks the parousia is imminent, but when it occurs those who are still alive will have no advantage over those who died. The scenario of that return is composed of traditional Israelite motifs (command, archangel's call, trumpet sound, clouds, etc.) found in other literature of this nature. The main point is to highlight the initiative of God. Just as God has raised Jesus, so will God raise those who believe in him. In the end, all will be with the Lord forever. These are comforting thoughts which believers ought to repeat to each other as needed.

In the gospel (Matt 25:1-13), Jesus urges vigilance and preparedness, for no one knows the day or the hour. It dovetails well with Paul's consoling reflections which assume the end is imminent. Subsequent circumstances in Paul's life brought him face to face with death (2 Cor 1:8-10) and made him realize (1) he might die before the parousia and (2) the parousia might still be far off. One must always be prepared to meet God.

Thirty-Third Sunday in Ordinary Time
1 Thessalonians 5:1-6

The Day of the Lord is a fearsome image drawn from the prophetic tradition (e.g., Amos 5:18; Joel 2:1; Zeph 1:7). It is a day of darkness and gloom, of clouds, a day causing people to tremble. Lord in this phrase is God. Once again Paul, who seems to expect that day to occur very soon, reminds the Thessalonians that it will be sudden, like a thief in the night. People will become complacent, perhaps skeptical that tragedy is imminent. They say "peace and security" (see Jer 6:14; Ezek 13:10, 16), but inescapable disaster will strike.

Paul exhorts to vigilance using the images of light and darkness, familiar from the Bible (Job 22:11) and extra-biblical literature (*Test. Naph* 2:7-10). Among the documents found at Qumran, various versions of "The War Scroll" describe a final, end-time battle between the "sons of light" (us) and the "sons of darkness" (them). (The lectionary has translated Paul's similar phrases inclusively as "children of light" and "children of darkness.") Such language is intended to distinguish insiders from outsiders, believers in Jesus from all others who do not believe in him. Paul adds phrases which he himself may have coined: sons of the day and [sons] of the night, perhaps because his reflections on the day of the Lord do not seem to include a final battle. His principal point is that believers must remain vigilant, sober, alert, ever prepared.

One might consider Jesus' parable in today's gospel (Matt 25:14-30) as something of a variation on the epistle's theme. While Paul urges preparedness, the gospel parable suggests that one ought to be prepared for the return of the Master in the way the Master expects. Since Americans normally pay more attention to the future than the present, suddenness of the Day of the Lord might encourage Americans to be prepared now, at this moment.

Thirty-Fourth Sunday in Ordinary Time (Christ the King)
1 Corinthians 15:20-26, 28

The feast of Christ the King celebrates Jesus as the human model which served God in creating the first earthling "in the divine image and likeness" (Gen 1:26-27). God doesn't have a body; Jesus does. A philosophical dictum asserts that "the first thing thought of is the last thing to occur" *(prima in intentione, ultima in executione)*. One thinks of baking a cake, but one must first gather the ingredients, mix and bake them. Eventually the cake, the first thing one thought of, emerges from the oven. So God thought first of an incarnate Son, Jesus, and in the course of time, Jesus was born.

Today's verses from 1 Corinthians form part of Paul's extended reflection on the resurrection. The Corinthians denied the resurrection (1 Cor 15:12-19 states their position), but Paul affirms it most emphatically (1 Cor 15:20-28). Jesus' status as "first fruits" means that what God has done for Jesus, God can and will do the same for others. We are associated with Adam by nature but with Jesus by free choice. Adam dealt us all death, Jesus bestows life. In his risen status, Jesus as Lord continues to destroy the forces hostile to authentic human existence: sovereignty, authority, and power (v. 25). The final enemy to be definitely conquered is Death. Once Jesus has accomplished all this when history comes to its end, he will return to his Father the authority once bestowed upon him to save all human kind. "All are yours, you are Christ's, and Christ is God's" (1 Cor 3:23).

Matthew (25:31-46) depicts that moment in today's gospel. A common and noteworthy thread linking the two readings is a focus on the body. Resurrection pertains to the body, just as do nourishment, clothing, and the like. This is a feast for celebrating the human body, an incredible gift from a God who is pure spirit. Perhaps this explains why so many corporeal peak experiences seem to point beyond the present, limited body to the transformed body of the resurrection. The gospel exhorts us to help one another enjoy bodily life in the present in hopes of achieving transformed corporeal existence in the future.

Recommended Resources

Elliott, John H. "Disgraced Yet Graced: The Gospel According to 1 Peter in the Key of Honor and Shame." *Biblical Theology Bulletin* 25 (1995) 166–78.

Malina, Bruce J., and Jerome H. Neyrey. *Portraits of Paul: An Archaeology of Ancient Personality.* Louisville, Ky.: Westminster John Knox Press, 1996.

Murphy-O'Connor, Jerome. *Paul: A Critical Life.* New York and Oxford: Oxford University Press, 1997.

_____. *Paul the Letter-Writer: His World, His Options, His Skills.* Collegeville: The Liturgical Press, 1995.

Neyrey, Jerome H. *Paul in Other Words: A Cultural Reading of His Letters.* Louisville, Ky.: Westminster John Knox Press, 1994.

Pilch, John J. *The Cultural Dictionary of the Bible.* Collegeville: The Liturgical Press, 1999.

_____. *The Cultural World of Jesus Sunday by Sunday: Cycle A.* Collegeville: The Liturgical Press, 1995.

_____. *Galatians and Romans.* The Collegeville Bible Commentary 6. Collegeville: The Liturgical Press, 1982.

_____. "Illuminating the World of Jesus through Cultural Anthropology." *The Living Light* 31 (1994) 20–31. http://www.georgetown. edu/faculty/pilchj/ click on: "Mediterranean Culture."

_____. *The Triduum: Breaking Open the Scriptures.* Collegeville: The Liturgical Press, 2000.

Sloyan, Gerard S. "What Kind of Canon Do the Lectionaries Constitute?" *Biblical Theology Bulletin* 30 (2000) 27–35.

Websites

Roman Catholic Lectionary for Mass:
http://clawww.lmu.edu/faculty/fjust/Lectionary.htm

Revised Common Lectionary:
http://divinity.library.vanderbilt.edu/lectionary